HOW TO
SPEAK
LIKE THE WORLD'S TOP
PUBLIC SPEAKERS

The Secrets Used By Some Of The
Greatest Speakers To Educate, Move
and Transform Their Audiences

RON MALHOTRA

Interior design: Ida Jansson

National Library of Australia Cataloguing-in-Publication data:
How To Speak Like The World's Top Public Speakers/ Ron Malhotra
Success/Self-help

ISBN: 978-0-6489376-7-8 (sc)
ISBN: 978-0-6489376-6-1 (e)

CONTENTS

CHAPTER TWO:

Glossophobia: The Fear of Public Speaking

CHAPTER THREE:

CHAPTER FOUR:

INTRODUCTION

"You are not being judged, the value of what you are bringing to the audience is being judged."

SETH GODIN

Amy is the valedictorian of her class. She has always looked forward to her graduation ceremony and finally it's tomorrow. She has written her valedictory speech, recounting her academic journey and that of her classmates. As she rehearses her lines, she can't help but marvel at the power of her words, their depth, the emotions they convey. However, she is nervous.

She wonders how she is going to read out this

speech without stuttering or quivering to the hundreds of people that would gather at the ceremony. Just thinking about tomorrow makes her palms sweaty and her tongue dry. Her YouTube search history shows the videos of speakers she admires—Barack Obama, Bernice King, Brian Tracy, Mel Robbins, Gary Vaynerchuk, Tony Robbins, Paula White, Oprah Winfrey, Deepak Chopra. She admires their composure, the way words glide off their tongue, the measured rhythm of their speeches. And she wonders if she could ever be like them.

Tomorrow is the big day. Tomorrow, for five minutes the audience will look up to her to tell a story. For five minutes her family, friends, and professors will listen to her with admiration. For five minutes she will be required to take her classmates through a journey of nostalgia. Amy doesn't want to disappoint, so she leans on hope, wishing that those five minutes won't turn out to be the most embarrassing moments of her life.

Amy's story above mirrors the reality of many— from valedictorians, to athletes, to a staff member required to pitch an idea to a board of directors. The

National Institute of Mental Health puts the figure at 73%—that is, 73% of the population suffer from public speaking anxiety, or glossophobia. The fear of public speaking ranks ahead of other well-known phobias like thanatophobia (fear of death), acrophobia (fear of heights), and arachnophobia (fear of spiders).

People with glossophobia are not worried about what to say; they are concerned about how to say it and what their audience will think. This is why it is considered a social anxiety disorder since the individual is *more* concerned about the audience's perception of them.

A writer once told me that what he fears about fame is the publicity and interviews that come with it. He prefers to hide behind the written word where he is only a still voice in the head of the reader. He said he wasn't sure whether he could be on live television without stammering embarrassingly through an interview. This made me realize that the fear of public speaking is much deeper than I thought.

When I am to speak to an audience, I am motivated by the value I have to offer. This is the only thing I think about, so I do all that is within my power to convey my message in the most effective way, ensuring that my value isn't diluted along the way. But this is not so for the glossophobic. In their case, the motivation to offer value is overwhelmed by something much bigger, and this may stem from physiology, thoughts, situations, or skills, as stated by Theo Tsaousides in a *Psychology Today* article.

So I figured that, while I may not fully understand the struggles of the glossophobic (since public speaking comes naturally to me), I can, through the methods outlined in this book, help them overcome their fears and stop hiding behind the written word, like my writer friend. In this book, I have outlined strategies that will transform you from the shy person plagued by stage fright to the individual filled with enough confidence and zeal to share their thoughts on any stage, irrespective of the audience and their numbers.

Also, this book is not for the glossophobic alone; it is for people who may not be glossophobic but do not possess the qualities for effective public speaking. They are not afraid to get on stage per se, but after delivering their speech, it seems to come out flat. This is because they lack the techniques required for excellent speech delivery. If you are such a person you need not to worry anymore, because you now hold in your hands the secrets towards mastering the art of public speaking.

These strategies have worked for me and I am *certain* that they will work for you, too. In fact, this book is an expansion of an article I wrote with the same title—"How to Speak Like The World's Top Public Speakers"—published in *The North-East Affairs*. In the article, I outlined eight tips for effective public speaking. However, I felt that there were nuances that I needed to explore—nuances so broad in scope that they cannot be summed up in an online article. So, this is why you now have this book in your hands. This book will teach you:

Chapter One: The Origin and Evolution of Public Speaking

Humans have always depended on words to communicate, inform, educate, liberate and empower. Suffice it to say, public speaking is as old as humankind. This chapter will show you the origins and evolution of public speaking, and its impact on humankind.

Chapter Two: Glossophobia: The Fear of Public Speaking

This chapter will take you through an in-depth exposition of glossophobia—what it is, its triggers, its impact on an individual, and the solutions to it.

Chapter Three: How To Speak Like The World's Top Public Speakers

For every venture in life there are strategies for success. This also applies to public speaking. To be a good public speaker, there are tips you need to know. You also need to know what the best public speakers do and what makes them highly sought after. This is what this chapter will show you.

Chapter Four: Some of The World's Top Public Speakers In Recent Times

A budding writer doesn't only know the general guidelines for writing, they also follow and study the specific skills of accomplished writers. In the same way, as an aspiring public speaker it is necessary you take note of the *specific* skills of some of the world's top public speakers today. This chapter will look into the performance of some of these speakers and what makes them stand out in the world of public speaking.

How To Use This Book

My books are geared towards offering strategies for success in any endeavor. This book isn't just another motivational piece; it is a guide, a manual, a textbook for public speaking. So study the tips outlined. Digest them. Make notes. Highlight points of relevance to you so you can reference them easily in the future.

In addition, I have listed some of the top public speakers the world has known. Some are long gone, while some are still living. Beyond this book, I expect you to study their speeches and speech delivery. Read more about them and their public speaking careers. Watch, digest, and learn from their videos.

It is my expectation that this book and the valuable tips herein will put you on the path to becoming a great public speaker.

CHAPTER ONE

The Origin and Evolution of Public Speaking

"God, that all-powerful Creator of nature and architect of the world, has impressed man with no character so proper to distinguish him from other animals, as by the faculty of speech."

QUINTILIAN

There are numerous debates as to the exact time in history when humankind developed speech, however, these debates all point to one conclusion: long before humans learnt how to write, they knew how to speak. What distinguishes us from other animals is that we have well-developed oral languages, and for centuries we have depended on these languages for communication, information, and education.

As I pondered the history of public speaking, I came to the conclusion that public speaking birthed because humans needed to persuade, liberate, and empower. Brett & Kate McKay confirmed my thoughts in their article, "Classical Rhetoric 101: A Brief History." In this article they note that rhetoric—which was later called public speaking—became a high art with the rise of Greek democracy. What this means is that the people of old depended on speech and public speaking as a tool for persuasion, liberation, and empowerment.

Therefore, it is impossible to discuss the history of public speaking without briefly journeying back to ancient Greece.

Public Speaking in the Classical Period (500 BCE – 400 BCE)

Public Speaking in Ancient Greece

"It is absurd to hold that a man should be ashamed of an inability to defend himself with his limbs, but not ashamed of an inability to defend himself with speech and reason; for the use of rational speech is more distinctive of a human being than the use of his limbs."

ARISTOTLE

Peter DeCaro stated that public speaking originated in Greece more than 2,500 years ago where it was first referred to as *rhetoric*. According to Peter, public speaking became a way of life for the Greeks at that time, just like football and baseball are to us today. Brett & Kate McKay gave the reason for this culture when they wrote: "Because Athenian democracy marshaled every free male into politics, every Athenian man had to be ready to stand in the Assembly and speak to persuade his countrymen to vote for or against a particular piece of legislation."

Unlike today's politics where money and modern technology are used to fuel various propaganda for or against a politician, the ancient Greeks had only their words. It was a battle of words. Thus, they had no choice but to develop public speaking into an art. In *Ancient History Encyclopedia*, Mark Cartwright wrote that in the assembly of Athens, any male citizen 18 years or over *could speak* and vote in the assembly. He further stated that about 3,000 people in the Greek population actively participated in politics, and of this number, only three sets of citizens dominated the political arena: the wealthiest, the most influential, and *the best speakers*. Peter DeCaro also wrote in his account of rhetoric in ancient Greece that, "public speaking was an Olympic event, where the winner received an olive wreath and was paraded through his town like a hero. Thus, Athens became a city of words, a city dominated by the orator." It was for this reason men like Thucydides and Aristophanes criticized democracy.

According to Mark Cartwright, Thucydides and Aristophanes were wary of democracy because the citizens could easily be swayed by good orators—or demagogues—who could appeal to their emotions. Although Aristotle did not criticize democracy, he understood the position of critics like Thucydides and Aristophanes because of a group of political actors known as the sophists. George Briscoe Kerferd, a Professor Emeritus of Greek, described the sophists as Greek lecturers, writers, and teachers who traveled around Greece giving instruction in a wide range of subjects in return for fees. They were among the sages of early Greek societies.

The *Standard Encyclopedia of Philosophy* notes that the rise of sophists was a response to the social, economic, political, and cultural developments of that time. They further stated that Greek cities experienced increasing wealth and intellectual sophistication at that period, which "created a demand for higher education beyond the traditional basic grounding in literacy, arithmetic, music and physical training." The sophists were responsible for meeting this demand and propagating a new kind of knowledge and skill. Brett & Kate tell us that sophists usually moved from city to city teaching young men how to speak and debate. And because public speaking was essential for a successful political life, people were willing to pay handsomely for the tutoring.

Documented histories about the Greek sophists all point to one fact: they were masters of the spoken word, and it was not long before they used this skill dishonestly. This was to Aristotle's great annoyance. According to Brett & Kate, Aristotle (and Plato) condemned the sophists for using emotions to persuade their audience at the expense of truth. They often focused on style and presentation, tricking the audience with "confusing analogies, flowery metaphors, and clever wordplay," even with subjects they had no prior knowledge of.

Aristotle was not the type of man who identified and complained about a problem without presenting a solution. He was an academic descendant of the famous philosophers of that era: he studied rhetoric under Plato, who studied under Socrates, who studied under Aspasia of Miletus. So while he exposed the abuse and misuse of rhetoric by the sophists, he also decided to show and teach the citizens what rhetoric actually is and should be. This birthed his treatise,

The Art of Rhetoric. The treatise was Aristotle's holistic approach to explore the nuances of rhetoric and public speaking, taking into consideration various elements like reasoning, prose style, character, and emotions. He developed a system for rhetoric which spanned centuries and influenced cultures. (This system is also highly influential in today's world and we will look at this later in the book as a guide towards effective public speaking.) Brett & Kate noted that Roman rhetoricians like Cicero and Quintilian often referenced Aristotle's treatise.

Public Speaking in Ancient Rome

> *"In an orator . . . we demand the acuteness
> of a logician, the profundity of a philosopher,
> the diction of a poet, the memory of a lawyer,
> the voice of a performer in tragic drama, the
> gestures, you might almost say, of an actor at
> the very top of his profession."*

CICERO

The Greeks greatly influenced the Romans. This is why they share similarities in their culture, mythology, and architecture. Rhetoric was also part of Greece's sphere of influence. However, rhetoric was still considered the heritage of the Greeks until they were conquered by the Romans.

Just as in Greece, rhetoric was fundamental to the politics of ancient Rome. Peter DeCaro pointed out that the Senate was the only permanent governing body and the only place where debates were allowed. And for one to debate, one had to know and employ "the persuasive art of rhetoric and oratory."

Rhetoric and oratory were not only important in Roman politics but also in the judiciary. Matthew Dillon & Lynda Garland in their book, *Ancient Rome: From the Early Republic to the Assassination of Julius Caesar* stated that, at the age of 15, children were taught rhetoric: they learnt the art of declamation through the practice of suasoriae (the presentation of historical or imaginary cases) and controversiae (court) cases. Gradually, many devoted themselves to rhetoric in order to defend themselves and acquire a fine reputation.

The Romans learnt rhetoric from the Greeks, however, they modified the art and introduced their own concepts. For instance, while the rhetoric of the Greeks tilted towards logic and reasoning, the Romans incorporated stylistic flourishes, captivating stories, and compelling metaphors (Brett & Kate McKay, 2010). Just as Aristotle was instrumental to the understanding and development of rhetoric in Greece, so too were Cicero and Quintilian instrumental to the development of rhetoric in Rome.

Cicero (106 – 43 BCE) was a statesman, lawyer,

scholar, philosopher, writer, and orator. Although born into a wealthy family, he gained influence because of his ability to, according to John Balsdon's account in *Britannica*, "evoke a wide range of emotions in plebeians and patricians alike." He evidenced the power of rhetoric and oratory in two major events which I have extracted from John Balsdon's account. First, in 80 or early 79 BCE, Cicero defended Sextus Roscius who was falsely accused of killing his father. This brilliant defense cemented his reputation at the bar. About the second time Cicero displayed his mastery in rhetoric. Balsdon wrote: "In 63 BCE Marcus Tullius Cicero gave an impassioned oration to his fellow senators that charged Catiline [a Roman aristocrat and democrat] with plotting to stage a violent coup. This so moved the Senate that they voted to implement martial law and execute the conspirators." Balsdon tagged this as Cicero's greatest achievement.

Being so good at rhetoric and oratory (in fact, Brett & Kate credited him as the first master rhetorician Rome produced), it was only logical that Cicero wrote treatises on the subject. The most popular of his works are: *De Inventione* (*About the Composition of*

Arguments), *De Oratore ad Quintum fratrem libri tres* (*On the Orator, Three Books for my Brother Quintus*), and *Topica* (*Topics*). In *De Inventione*, Cicero explained that there are Five Canons of Rhetoric: Invention, Arrangement, Style or Expression, Memory, and Delivery. (We will revisit these canons in detail later in this book.) Cicero's writings guided schools on the subject of rhetoric from medieval times to the Renaissance, even down to present day.

Regarding his style of oratory, Balsdon said that Cicero was a fluid speaker—"drifting between florid and concise language" like his instructor, Molon of Rhodes. He relied on "cadence, emotion, the energy of his audience and interweaving references to literature, philosophy and history." By connecting literature, philosophy and history to his speeches, Cicero practiced what he taught. According to Brett and Kate, Cicero was of the opinion that for one to be persuasive, one had to be knowledgeable in history, politics, art, literature, ethics, law, and medicine. He noted that by being a liberally educated man he would be better able to connect with any audience he addressed. It is not erroneous to assert that when Quintilian stated that "the mind is exercised by the variety and multiplicity of the subject matter. . ." he was corroborating Cicero's stance.

Quintilian (35 – 100 AD) arrived about a hundred years after Cicero had long gone, however his ideas on rhetoric were invaluable and consolidated Cicero's. However, he wasn't like his predecessor; for, while Cicero was multifaceted, Quintilian was mainly a teacher of rhetoric (although he had had a stint in the courtroom). Martin Clarke records in *Britannica* that Quintilian became the first teacher to receive a state salary for teaching Latin rhetoric and held the position of Rome's leading teacher until he retired in 88 AD.

One may wonder why Quintilian became an authority in rhetoric when Cicero had already taught and written exhaustively on the subject over a hundred years before. Peter DeCaro provides a viable reason for this, writing that: "During the hundred plus years which elapsed between the death of Cicero and the birth of Quintilian, education had spread all over the Roman Empire, with rhetoric as it's key focus. But by Quintilian's time, the popular oratorical trend was not rhetoric in the traditional sense, but 'silver Latin,' a style that favored ornate embellishment over clarity and precision." Therefore, he had to re-concentrate what had been diluted, or, as DeCaro put it, "react against this trend." To do this, he published his famous treatise, *Institutio Oratoria* (*Institutes of Oratory*).

This twelve-volume textbook exhaustively covered all aspects of rhetoric. It even expounded Cicero's five canons of rhetoric. According to DeCaro, the treatise advocated the return to simpler and clearer language. Just like Cicero's treatises, Quintilian's *Institutio Oratoria* became an instructional instrument for rhetoricians of the Middle Ages and Renaissance.

Public Speaking in the Middle Ages
(400 CE – 1400 CE)

"This, of course, is eloquence in teaching,
whereby the result is attained in speaking, not
that what was distasteful becomes pleasing,
nor that what one was unwilling to do is done,
but that what was obscure becomes clear."

ST. AUGUSTINE

(The Middle Ages is often referred to as a dark and culturally empty period. There are many reasons for this, but to understand these reasons, one would need to engage an in-depth study of the history of those times.)

Despite the seemingly "dark emptiness" of the Middle Ages, a system that has become perpetually significant sprouted up in those times—namely, Religion. Religion was the central feature of the Middle Ages, and people relied on rhetoric to propagate their faith—just like the religious leaders of today. "Instead of being a tool to lead the state, rhetoric was seen as a means to save souls," (Brett & Kate McKay, 2010).

I consider this was a good thing, the diversification of rhetoric into religion, which was a new system at that time. However, it is surprising that religion, particularly Christianity, tried to bite the hand that fed it. Peter DeCaro wrote that as Christianity grew in power, it considered rhetoric a pagan art and condemned the study of it. The Christian faithful of the time were of the opinion that "one's belief in Christian truth brought with it the ability to communicate that truth effectively." I would like to think that it was for this reason that there weren't as many rhetoricians in the Middle Ages as there were in ancient Greece and Rome. The only poster child for rhetoric in the Middle Ages was St. Augustine, who according to DeCaro was a teacher of rhetoric before converting to Christianity.

Many historians have described St. Augustine as a man of high intellectual capacity. James O'Donnell in his *Britannica* biography of the man himself, wrote that St. Augustine is "perhaps the most significant Christian thinker after St. Paul." However, *Mere Rhetoric*, a podcast supported by the University of

Texas' Humanities Media Project points out that having taught rhetoric for ten to fifteen years, St. Augustine was probably conflicted on how to marry the *persuasive* emphasis of rhetoric to the *inspiration-based* doctrine of his new faith. Mere Rhetoric wrote: "He must have spent a lot of time pondering the question of how his previous career (as one who taught other people how to persuade) could be reconciled with his new religion's emphasis on inspiration. If God will give the preacher exactly the words which he needs, either through scripture or through divine inspiration, is there any space for a Christian rhetoric?"

St. Augustine's ponderings made him stand out from other Christians who totally condemned rhetoric because of their (new) faith. In fact, in Lumen Learning's public speaking course, "The History of Public Speaking," they stated that St. Augustine believed the study of persuasion to be a worthwhile pursuit for the church. This was what birthed his own treatise, *De doctrina christiana* (*On Christian Doctrine*)—a text of four books that elucidated on how to interpret and teach the scriptures. With this work, St. Augustine reconfigured the minds of Christians towards the importance of rhetoric. DeCaro notes what St. Augustine asserted about human beings, in that they "needed to understand rhetoric in order to explain the Christian message, and then be able to teach it to others. He believed every Christian was obligated to spread Christ's message; thus, rhetoric became an obligation to every Christian."

We can comfortably posit that when it comes to rhetoric, St. Augustine became the bridge between the classical era and the medieval era. A man who strove to preserve the tenets of rhetoric and public speaking, ensuring its survival well into the Renaissance. Little wonder then, that St. Augustine is sometimes referred to as "the last classical man and the first medieval man."

Public Speaking in the Renaissance
(1400 – 1600 CE)

"A speech comes alive only if it rises from the heart, not if it floats on the lips."
DESIDERIUS ERASMUS

I consider the Renaissance the most interesting period in human history. In it was an explosion of literature, science and fine arts which paved the way for modern civilization. The era was blessed with some of the finest thinkers and authors (Francesco Petrarca, Francis Bacon, René Descartes, William Shakespeare), scientists (Nicolaus Copernicus, Galileo Galilei, Johannes Kepler, Isaac Newton), painters and sculptors (Leonardo da Vinci, Giovanni Bellini, Michelangelo, Giorgione) the world has ever known.

Unlike in the classical and medieval eras where rhetoric was applied only to law and politics (and religion), Richard Nordquist, citing the words of

Heinrich F. Plett, said that during the Renaissance, rhetoric wasn't confined to a single occupation but covered a wide range of theoretical and practical activities like scholarship, politics, education, philosophy, history, science, ideology, and literature. Furthermore, the style of rhetoric received attention during the Renaissance from scholars such as Petrus Ramus and Francis Bacon who, according to Lumen Learning, challenged much of what early scholars thought of truth, ethics, and morals as they applied it to communication as a whole.

The Renaissance brimmed with a new kind of intelligentsia, unlike the medieval era. Of the Renaissance, DeCaro wrote: "[it was] a major revolt against an intellectually barren medieval spirit, and especially against scholasticism, in favor of intellectual freedom. A hunger developed for all things classical." And *all things classical* included rhetoric. Cicero's and Quintilian's texts were rediscovered and used in rhetoric courses. For instance, Quintilian's *De Inventione* became a standard rhetoric textbook at most European universities. Francesco Petrarca spearheaded the rediscovery of Cicero's texts, and one of the texts he found, *Brutus*, became one of the most important books in the Renaissance (Brett & Kate McKay, 2010; Peter A. DeCaro, n.d.). Brett & Kate further remarked that Renaissance scholars wrote their own treatises and books on the subject and emphasized applying rhetorical skill to one's own vernacular instead of Latin or ancient Greek. This emphasis was a fundamental aspect of Ramism.

Ramism was a collection of theories formed from the teachings of Petrus Ramus—a French philosopher, rhetorician, and logician—on rhetoric, logic, and pedagogy. Actually, Ramus subtracted from rhetoric instead of adding to it. If we were to follow the path of Ramism, the art of public speaking wouldn't be as appealing as it is today. Peter DeCaro noted that Ramus placed rhetoric under logic and took away two of its key Ciceronian canons (invention and organization), leaving it with only style and delivery. James Veazie Skalnik in his book, *Ramus and Reform: University and Church at the End of the Renaissance*, describes this with more imagery. He writes: "The decline of rhetoric as an academic discipline was due at least in part to [the] emasculation of ancient art [by French logician Peter Ramus] . . . Rhetoric was henceforth to be a handmaiden of logic, which would be the source of discovery and arrangement. The art of rhetoric would simply dress that material in ornate language and teach orators when to raise their voices and extend their arms to the audience." Thankfully, Ramism was discarded during the Enlightenment Era.

Public Speaking in the Enlightenment Period (1600 – 1800 CE)

> *"Rhetoric is a powerful instrument of error and deceit."*
> **JOHN LOCKE**

The slang, "woke" describes the *awareness* of issues today, especially those pertaining to social and racial justice. It also loosely implies one's desire to search, seek out truth for oneself, instead of founding one's own ideas on preexisting norms. This current generation may have coined the word, but the origins and idea of "staying woke" began with the people of The Enlightenment Era.

The people — the thinkers — of this era *revolutionized* European politics, philosophy, science, and communications by questioning traditional authority and embracing the notion that humanity could be improved through rational change (**www. history.com**, 2009). Traditional rhetoric was not left out in this revolution. As a matter of fact, it underwent a journey of criticisms and modifications between the 17th and 18th centuries, as noted by Bruce Herzberg & Patricia Bizzell in their book, *The Rhetorical Tradition: Readings from Classical Times to the Present.*

Herzberg & Bizzell recount that when the concept of logic was changed, the concept of traditional rhetoric was *indirectly* affected. Logic was a branch of knowledge on which rhetoric had its foundation, based on the Ramistic doctrines. Changing the concept of logic was the first influence of the scientific and philosophical revolutions on rhetoric. But the concept of logic wasn't just changed; rhetoric was reinstated, and the five Ciceronian canons became the foundation of rhetorical study. Traditional rhetoric sustained its relevance and even branched into other subjects like history, poetry, literary criticism, music, drama, gardening, and architecture (Herzberg & Bizzell, 2001; Peter DeCaro, n.d.). This was known as the '*belles lettres*' movement, a French term that translates as "beautiful letters."

However, since the Enlightenment Era was a period defined by intellectual radicalism and continuous cultural reformations, it wasn't long before traditional rhetoric came under fire again. This time it was attacked by the adherents of new science. Herzberg & Bizzell note that, "they claimed that rhetoric obscured the truth by encouraging the use of ornamented rather than plain, direct language." Philosophers called for language reforms. The church and influential writers supported it too. And soon perspicuity—clarity— became the accepted style for speaking.

Perspicuity was a concept that was in line with what John Locke believed rhetoric should be. Locke was not a rhetorician, but a philosopher who contributed greatly to the subject of epistemology. He believed that the goals of rhetoric were to teach, to entertain, and to persuade—goals which are fulfilled through language (thelockedown.weebly.com). In his words, language should be used "first, to make known one man's thoughts or ideas to another; secondly to do it with as much ease and quickness as is possible; and thirdly to convey the knowledge of things." Locke's ideas on rhetoric harmoniously correlated with those of his predecessor, Francis Bacon.

According to Herzberg & Bizzell, Bacon also advocated a plain style; however, he was of the opinion that rhetoric applies reason to the imagination to move the will, and, for him, "reasoning was not enough to achieve persuasion; in order to teach people or move them to action one had to address all the faculties." Also, Bacon subscribed to the art of eloquence in rhetoric, but it was not until the early eighteenth century that elocution became a movement in and of itself.

Elocution as an emergent movement became focused on delivery and provided instructions for bodily actions such as gestures, facial expressions, tone, and correct pronunciation in an era concerned only with correctness. It also analyzed nonverbal appeals to emotions which were hitherto neglected (Herzberg & Bizzell, 2001; Lumen Learning, n.d.). But what gave elocutionists their strength ironically became the end of the movement. Peter DeCaro stated that because of the shifting focus towards delivery and eloquence, the public began to see rhetoric as "empty, insincere speaking that hid behind the mask of sophistication." This sadly led to the decline of rhetoric as a major subject of study and teaching. Rhetoric could no longer be regarded as a multidisciplinary art and was this time placed under the study of the English language. However, this would change by the early 1900s.

The Enlightenment period embraced other notable contributors to rhetoric whose works still influence contemporary studies of public speaking today. These contributors include George Campbell, a Scottish minister, theologian, and philosopher of rhetoric who wrote the book, *Philosophy of Rhetoric*; and his countryman, Hugh Blair, a minister, teacher, and rhetorician who penned *Lectures on Rhetoric and Belles Lettres*.

Public Speaking in Contemporary Times (1900 till date)

*"A good speech should be like a woman's skirt;
long enough to cover the subject and short
enough to create interest."*
WINSTON CHURCHILL

Public speakers in the 20th and 21st centuries followed and built on the template that already existed. They put into the practice Aristotelian and Ciceronian theories, plus theories from other scholars of the classical, renaissance, and enlightenment eras. Also, the development of mass media heightened the need for rhetoric. With the advent of televisions, radios, photography and film, coupled with sociopolitical issues like racism, public speaking gained greater relevance. Politicians, clerics, and activists understood that they could use mass media to reach a large number of people and appeal to their emotions at the same time.

Therefore, there came the need to aggregate all the principles of rhetoric and public speaking and promote its study in schools. Peter DeCaro notes that, in 1914, a body known as the Speech Communication Association was formed with the aim of restoring the rich qualities and scope that had once been attributed to rhetoric. Lumen Learning's "History of Public Speaking" also lends credence to this: they state that in the twentieth century, rhetoric was a concentrated field of study with rhetorical courses established in high schools and universities. These courses (e.g. public speaking and speech analysis) applied fundamental Greek theories and also included topics such as classical rhetoric and contemporary rhetoric, alongside empirical and qualitative social science.

Some of the greatest public speakers in the twentieth century were heavily influenced by classical rhetoricians. For instance, Stephen Johnson noted in a blog post (where he looked into the lives of seven of the greatest public speakers in history), that Winston Churchill employed the highest and most magnificent command of the English language, especially through the use of short words, Anglo-Saxon words, and

Shakespearean words, which were often accompanied by the most powerful of deliveries. Furthermore, Johnson described John F. Kennedy as one who had the "ability to speak as if he were having an authentic conversation with an audience, as opposed to lecturing them." Although Adolf Hitler is considered one of the most villainous men to have ever lived, yet Johnson makes a point to note that he of all men understood the importance of mastering the art of public speaking as critical to his success. Hitler was known to have practiced facial expressions and gestures while weaving metaphors and abstract ideas into his political speeches. Another famous public speaker was Martin Luther King Jr., who Johnson describes as having a "strong musicality" to his speeches. MLK's famous speech, "I Have a Dream," was heavily influenced by Shakespeare, the Bible, as well as many civil rights thinkers.

Today, the internet and social media have made mastering the art of public speaking easier. In some cases, contemporary speakers do not need to use words to evoke emotions or create images in the minds of the audience, since now they can employ the use of visual and audiovisual technologies to amplify the strength of their words. But these technologies are not meant to replace the core techniques or principles of public speaking; they are only sufficient in terms of adding to its artistic quality. Therefore, it is an important task for the beginning public speaker to learn to master the rudiments of public speaking without any depending on the additives.

Rhetoric, Oratory, and Public Speaking

"Those orators who give us much noise and many words, but little argument and less wit, and who are the loudest when least lucid, should take a lesson from the great volume of nature; she often gives us the lightning without the thunder, but never the thunder without the lightning."

ELIHU BURRITT

The purpose of exploring the history of rhetoric is to highlight the dynamics of public speaking. The scholars of the classical, renaissance and enlightenment eras shaped public speaking into what it is today and provides a framework upon which the art can be learned. Throughout our exposition on the evolution of public speaking, we discover that the word "rhetoric" was mostly used to identify the art of effective communication. Although used interchangeably with "public speaking," rhetoric is the broader term.

Rhetoric is commonly defined as the art of using language to persuade. This can be achieved through public speaking, writing, poetry, advertising, politics and various other media. From the classical era to the enlightenment era, rhetoric was synonymous with public speaking. This was because oral speech was the major medium used to deliver persuasive arguments in different sectors, from politics to religion. However, to persuade effectively, a speaker had to have a key trait: oratory.

Oratory is the art of effectively delivering speeches especially in a forceful and expressive manner. The speech may have the right words, but it is the oratory that captures the attention of the audience. On the power of oratory, Craig Baird, a Professor of Speech at the University of Iowa, noted that, in Martin Luther King Jr.'s speech "I Have a Dream" oratorical skills were applied to "appeal for further rights for U.S blacks to an intensity that galvanized millions."

The key elements of oratory according to Baird, are: a speaker; an audience; a background of time, place and other conditions; a message; a transmission by voice, articulation, and bodily accompaniments. Suffice it to say, oratory is the backbone of public speaking.

Today, rhetoric has taken on many forms. A rhetorical performance can be: An article. A book. A public speech. A sales copy. A manifesto. A sermon. A television Ad. As long as the work is aimed at persuasion, it is defined as rhetoric.

However, it is my belief that present day public speaking goes beyond persuasion; it involves inspiration, motivation, education and illumination. Persuasion implies speaking to an audience in order to change their minds, convince them about a particular view, or inspire them towards taking action. Some might say that motivation and inspiration achieves this too, but this is not totally correct.

Most of the time, the act of persuasion is aimed at changing the minds of the audience to take a course of action that benefits the speaker more than the audience. The politician who speaks in a rally uses persuasion as a tool to get the people to vote for him. If he succeeds, the populace will then cast their vote for a person who they aren't sure can live up to his promise. His speech may not have inspired or motivated them to be better versions of themselves, but it has certainly persuaded them to vote for him.

In the same vein, persuasion is a tool employed by sales personnel. As a matter of fact, copywriting and other selling techniques are deeply rooted in persuasion. The salesperson uses the spoken or written word to highlight a need to the prospective buyer, thereby persuading them to purchase their product or service. Whether the product or service actually adds value to the buyer depends on the integrity of the seller. But between the two parties, the person that benefits more here is the seller—he is the one who receives money, irrespective of whether or not the buyer finds the product or service useful.

Now, I am not saying that persuasion is wrong.

Not at all. As a matter of fact, persuasion is the main tool the worthy politician needs to convince the electorate that he is right for the job. It is also the tool the seller requires to introduce a person to a product that would be beneficial to them. All I am saying is that public speaking is more the tool, the conduit between the person and the product. The world's top public speakers are known because their words resonate with the people. They inspire them, show them something they've never known, and challenge them to be better.

For instance, Martin Luther King Jr. persuaded U.S blacks to demand their rights but he did this by: (1) *illuminating* their minds to the truth that they are not lesser beings because of their skin, (2) *inspiring* them towards hope, and (3) *teaching* the world that character, not skin, is the best yardstick for judging an individual.

Top public speakers deliver their message with confidence and poise. They know that the audience is watching and assessing if they are also convinced by the message they are passing on. Because how can persuasion be effective if the speaker's mannerisms exhibit doubt and fear? However, there are people who show fear while delivering a speech, and it's no fault of theirs. These people are only victims of a condition beyond their control. They love to speak, they want to speak—but they just cannot overcome their fear of public speaking.

CHAPTER TWO

Glossophobia: The Fear of Public Speaking

*"Courage is resistance to fear, mastery of
fear—not absence of fear."*
MARK TWAIN

I know that there are people who are not afraid to
speak in public, but they lack the know-how of public
speaking. However, I will not delve into showing how
to speak like the world's top public speakers without
first touching on the subject of glossophobia, which
is a major reason why many don't do well as public
speakers.

The word "glossophobia" was first used in 1964
(Merriam Webster Dictionary). It is a combination

of two words: "glosso" meaning tongue, language, speech; and "phobia" meaning fear. It is the fear of public speaking.

Glossophobia, also called speech anxiety, is classified as a social anxiety disorder. Just like in other phobias where there is an *unexplainable fear*, the glossophobic person experiences a fear so strong that it restricts the person from speaking in public. Lisa Fritscher states that glossophobia is a subset of social phobia; a condition where an individual is anxious about social interactions. She further remarks that *most* glossophobic persons do not show symptoms of other forms of social phobia, like fear of meeting new people, or fear of performing tasks in front of others. According to her, many glossophobic individuals can dance or sing on stage, as long as they don't speak.

Glossophobia is not just stage fright. Stage fright is one of the manifestations of glossophobia. I heard a story of a university student who competed for a position in his faculty. He was vivacious, spoke with everyone, laughed with everyone. The students rooted for him as the date for the debate against his opponent drew near. But on that day, seeing the audience, he suddenly became paralyzed with stage fright. To embolden himself, he went backstage to smoke cigarettes and drink alcohol.

I also heard of a drummer who had no problem playing before a crowd. But anytime he was handed the mic to speak on behalf of the band, he froze. One day, a band member asked him why he had no problem playing the drums before a huge crowd but couldn't speak to that same crowd. The drummer responded, saying that by playing the drums, he was able to hide behind the cymbals. No one could see him. He was just alone in his own world at that moment, playing, nodding his head to the metallic groove of the music.

These stories show that for some people, it is not being on stage that is the problem; the problem is speaking on stage. No matter the number of people, they just cannot speak in public. They are crippled by the fear of knowing that people are watching and listening to them. In this age of social media, televisions,Instagram, Live/TV, Facebook Live—there are people who don't use these features to communicate with their audience. Although they realize that they are not on any stage, they are still filled with dread knowing that many Instagram or Facebook users are watching and listening. The symptoms of glossophobia flood their body: sweating, increased heartbeat, dry mouth, shortness of breath, tensed muscles, headache, and an urge to urinate. So they cower behind their fear, never to speak.

Many are comfortable with being glossophobic because they think it does not impact their lives in any way. But this is not true. Glossophobia can interfere with the individual's life, making them shy away from making key decisions, as a result, denying themselves real opportunities. Arlin Cuncic rightly notes that a glossophobic will change courses at college to avoid oral presentations, change jobs or careers to avoid uncomfortable presentations, decline to give speeches at major life events (such as delivering a best man's speech at a wedding), or even turn down promotions because of public speaking obligations.

The impacts of glossophobia can also be physiological. Dom Barnard states that extreme tension can develop in a person as a result of the mind being cluttered with thoughts, and that this can also affect the hearing of the glossophobic person. The glossophobic person can suffer from such things as intense anxiety, heart palpitations or increased heart rate, all of which can lead to high blood pressure and other negative physiological complications upon the body's system.

Although a phobia is defined as an unexplainable, often exaggerated fear of something, I believe there is always a basis for every fear. Fear does not exist in a vacuum. It is not the disease. It is the symptom. It is the manifestation of something deeper lurking in the background. Fear is often backed by an (un)known factor. A common meaning given to fear (which I note in my book, *The Success Answer*) is:

False **E**vidence **A**ppearing **R**eal.

For the evidence of fear to appear, there must be something presenting this evidence, some driving force behind it. Knowing what fuels your fuel is the first step towards overcoming it.

Reasons why people fear public speaking

> *"You gain strength, courage and confidence*
> *by every experience in which you really stop*
> *to look fear in the face. You are able to say to*
> *yourself, 'I have lived through this horror. I*
> *can take the next thing that comes along.' You*
> *must do the thing you think you cannot do."*
>
> **ELEANOR ROOSEVELT**

There are phobias that are understandable. Someone who has a fear of heights is scared of falling to their death. It is also understandable why anyone would be afraid of snakes. I think that everyone should be enabled by this innate, in-built fear because the reality is that snakes *are* deadly and fear lies at the core of our human makeup, as it works to protect us, and ensures our survival. This is a good fear. But there are other fears or phobias that are much more difficult to come to terms with. It is because of these phobias that the meaning of 'phobia' as a general term used across dictionaries includes the words "exaggerated" and "irrational," as their synonyms. Phobias like xenophobia (fear of strangers) and geliophobia (fear of laughter) are bizarre fears and incomprehensible to the human mind.

There is a tendency for me, as a public speaker, to consider glossophobia as an irrational fear. I mean, you are speaking to human beings, rational beings, not savages. They can't and won't harm you. They are only there to listen. However, over the years I have come to realize that when it comes to phobias, the sufferers are helpless. I know of people who *imagine* themselves speaking to a large crowd—giving an appreciation speech for, say, receiving an award, addressing a graduating crowd of students, or debating against political opponents. But when the time comes to do any of these things, they shrink. And it is not their fault.

From my personal studies and observations, I believe, there are a number of reasons why people fear public speaking. These reasons may be the result of physiological limitations, having self-esteem issues, negative thinking, pre-existing conditions, or lacking general skills.

Why people fear public speaking #1: Physiology

"The way you overcome shyness is to
become so wrapped up in something that
you forget to be afraid."
LADY BIRD JOHNSON

When the human body deviates from its normal physiological function, the first step is to examine the body to find out what the anomaly is. Is an organ malfunctioning? Are neurons misfiring? Is there an imbalance in the neurotransmitters somewhere? Is there a faulty gene? This examination is a primary step towards understanding all pathologies, even those like clinical depression, that are considered to be triggered mainly by environmental factors. Stephanie Faris reveals that a British research team isolated a gene that was found to be prevalent in more than 800 families with recurrent clinical depression.

Researchers have shown that there is a physiological basis to phobias like glossophobia. Theo Tsaousides explains that fear and anxiety arouses the autonomic nervous system in response to a threat. The autonomic nervous system is the control tower of the body that regulates body functions, like heartbeat and sexual arousal.

The autonomic nervous system uses fear as a positive signal to alert us to danger. However, we see a hyper-arousal of this system present in phobias when an individual perceives a situation as a threat. Ellen Dunnigan, the founder of *Accent On Business*, a public speaking and communication skills firm in Indiana, sheds more light on this. Dunnigan traces glossophobia to our ancient ancestors, whose fight or flight responses were stimulated in the presence of wooly mammoths. The limbic system is the part of the brain responsible for driving this response. And although our brains have evolved through the ages, the limbic system no longer only has wooly mammoths to contend with in its list of potential threats; nowadays the list has expanded itself to include dark alleys and public speaking.

And Dunnigan's explanation is compatible with Tsaousides's. According to Tsaousides, some researchers suggest that those who experience anxiety in different situations are more likely to be anxious about public speaking. He also notes that highly anxious people are less likely to conquer their fear of public speaking. In this case, it is not about speaking in public; it is about the fact that they are predisposed to fear and anxiety.

Furthermore, Zijing Sang points to genetics as another cause of glossophobia. Individuals with a family history of glossophobia (or a relatable fear) will likely end up showing signs of glossophobia. According to Sang, a glossophobic person may be very aware that their fear is irrational, but that "they have the least amount of power in controlling their feelings." In other cases they may even experience what researchers call anxiety sensitivity or '*the fear of fear.*'

> *"There is nothing to fear, but fear itself."*
> **FRANKLIN D. ROOSEVELT**

In describing anxiety sensitivity, Theo Tsaousides states that, in addition to their existent worry about public speaking, people with high anxiety sensitivity "also worry that they will be overwhelmingly anxious in front of their audience, and that they will come across as a shaky speaker." In other words, they are afraid of how their fear of public speaking might impact them and their performance on important occasions.

But there are times when people are scared of public speaking not because they are physiologically or genetically disadvantaged, but because they have a poor self image.

Why people fear public speaking #2: Low Self-esteem

"It's not what you are that is holding you back. It's what you think you are not."

ANONYMOUS

"People may flatter themselves just as much by thinking that their faults are always present to other people's minds, as if they believe that the world is always contemplating their individual charms and virtues."

ELIZABETH GASKELL

Many have failed to attain their goals simply because they limited by feelings of low self-worth. The issue of low self-esteem cuts across many activities. People who have low self-esteem always believe that they can never be good enough, nor do they believe they can they produce anything good. When it comes to public speaking, it becomes a whole soup of complexities. They feel insecure about their physical appearance, the sound of their voice, their words, gestures. And, they are always quick to always ask, "What if?"

- "What if my clothes aren't appealing?" You offer to style them, praise their gorgeousness, tell them they are beautiful. Yet they are still not satisfied, so they ask:
- "What if my voice sounds weird on the mic? What if I stutter?" You move to assure them that their voice sounds perfect, that they will not stutter, nor will their voice quiver. But they still ask:
- "What if my words don't make sense,

what if they don't resonate with the audience?" You tell them that you have gone through their speech, and you work to reassure them that the audience will be blown away by their words. But even when you think you've pumped up their confidence, they ask another question:

- "What if I don't convey the words with the right gestures? What if my body language makes the whole presentation boring?"

The questions are relentless and exhausting. It is an unending game of assurance and reassurance. A game in which the assurer has a slim chance of winning. The big problem with individuals with low self-esteem is that they do not ask these questions as a way to boost their confidence or work on themselves. They ask these questions not because they want to be (re)assured of their worth, but because they want to cement the belief and continue with the narrative that they are not good enough.

There are many factors that contribute towards low self-esteem, but I am going to speak to the ones that relate specifically to the individual's reluctance to speak in public. I culled this list from Suzanne Lachmann's *Psychology Today* article, "10 Sources of Low Self-Esteem."

Reasons why a person could have low self-esteem

Disapproving authority figures: An individual who grows up receiving no commendation from figures like parents or guardians may have a dampened self-worth. Such a person finds it difficult to believe that they can be good at any task, especially one that requires commanding the attention of an audience and addressing them. In Lachmann's words, "If you were criticized, no matter what you did or how hard you tried, it becomes difficult to feel confident and comfortable in your own skin. The shame that was forced on you for perpetually 'failing' can feel blindingly painful."

1. *Uninvolved/preoccupied caregivers*: Humans crave and need validation in their lives. We

need to hear, "Hey! I see what you are doing, and you are doing well. Keep it up." Thus, it is saddening when no one recognizes our efforts. Many children put hard work into their academics or talents to gain the approval of their parents. And there is a tendency for such children to have a deflated esteem when their parents do not even acknowledge their efforts. A person who grows up under such conditions will likely have the notion that they are unimportant, unheard, unnoticed, and unworthy. Lachmann says such feelings can result in the belief that one must continually for one's existence. So how can such a person ever be expected to speak in public, when their voice has already been so muted?

2. *Bullying*: Unfortunately, many people do not know the horrible impacts of bullying. Sadly, the bullied individual becomes so scarred that they end up always feeling unsafe around people. They build a wall of distrust around themselves. Since they do not have the gift of psychics to know the intentions of people

around them, they choose to shut everyone out. It gets worse if the bullying comes from within the home. These individuals will inevitably also distrust their audience and refrain from public speaking. Questions that infiltrate their minds might include, "What if I'm booed off the stage?" "What if they make fun of me?" The bullied victim is often plagued by such self doubts.

3. *Academic challenges without caregiver support*: There are people who think that failure in one aspect of their lives means failure in all aspects of their lives. Individuals who weren't book-smart growing up and whose parents never encouraged them may grow up to see themselves as underachievers who can't amount to any form of excellence. These individuals may be good at public speaking but they will forever question and doubt their capabilities. They doubt how they can succeed at public speaking when they couldn't make good grades in school. For instance, a boy who had poor grades in his English Literature

courses may find it ironic that he could later become a good public speaker. This distrust in the self becomes a proverbial clog in the wheel. Lachmann writes that such a person may excessively doubt their smartness and feel terribly self-conscious about sharing their opinions.

4. *Guilt and shame*: This usually happens in motivational speaking. A person may refrain from motivating or speaking to others because they feel they lack the emotional, moral or psychological justification to motivate or inspire. They are tied to their past, irrespective of the fact that they've changed for the better. An internet fraudster after serving his time in prison may lack the wherewithal to show others the ills of fraud. A sickle cell patient may not see herself as an inspiration and may be unwilling to inspire others to stay strong when she knows she fights pain every day and depends on drugs to have a semblance of health. A writer may not feel bold enough to lecture others on writing when there are

countless rejection letters sitting in his email. A victim of physical, sexual, or emotional abuse may not feel worthy enough to liberate others with their words because, as Lachmann says, they may have found ways to cope with the abuse, ways that are unhealthy, ways that make them view themselves as "repulsive and searingly shameful."

5. *The media*: Sometimes, what is meant to inspire us is actually what demotivates us. The internet has made information in all forms so easily accessible that we have called it 'living in the information age.' So it is easy to watch or listen to the greatest speeches the world has ever heard at the click of a button. But there are individuals who doubt their abilities so much that instead of listening to these speeches and saying, "I can speak like this guy someday," they would rather say, "I'll never attempt public speaking. I can never speak like that guy." Rather than *learning* from the best, these individuals *compare* themselves to the best. But a person can never receive value

from someone they compare themselves with. Comparison only breeds resentment or doubt. (For the individual with low self-esteem, it breeds the latter.) You either resent the person for being better than you, or doubt your ability to measure up to that person. In any case, you have just shut yourself out from the value you could have received.

The factors that predispose a person to low self-esteem inevitably alter the individual's thought processes. And once these thought processes become negative, the individual may end up glossophobic.

Why people fear public speaking #3: Thoughts

"I have always thought the actions of men the best interpreters of their thoughts."
JOHN LOCKE

"The worlds of thought and action overlap. What you think has a way of becoming true."
ROGER VON OECH

I am a writer, and I take time to interact with other writers. I spoke with a freelance writer a while back and he narrated his writing journey to me. He said he started out writing only flash fiction—one hundred words, five hundred words, or, the maximum, a thousand words. He told me he never accepted jobs that went beyond five thousand words because he never thought he would be able to write such volume. The bulkiness of, say, a work of ten thousand words scared him and he turned down such gigs. But one day, he was so broke and was faced with a writing gig of fifteen thousand words. He had to decide between remaining broke because he feared the volume of the job, or accepting the job and stretching his capacity. That day, he chose the latter. It birthed courage in him. He took up the job, delivered it within the scheduled timeframe, and ultimately impressed the client.

We underestimate the power in and of our thoughts. The mind is the seat of our thoughts. And thoughts are the powerhouse of actions. Every human action is powered by a thought, even involuntary actions. We wince and pull our hand back from a flame because we have hitherto processed in our minds that the flame causes pain. We didn't just think about wincing at that moment; our mind has already processed the thought in a nanosecond, relying either on our past experiences of a burning flame, or learning of its danger through warnings from others—and we have saved that thought and filed it away somewhere until the moment when it's needed.

When a person houses negative thoughts about public speaking (e.g. I cannot be a good speaker, I may come off as boring, I am scared of crowds, I will stutter, etc.), there is a strong tendency for such a person to become glossophobic. These thoughts dampen the can-do spirit in the individual. Theo Tsaousides notes that these thoughts arise "when people overestimate the stakes of communicating their ideas in front of others, viewing the speaking event as a potential threat to their credibility, image, and chance to reach an audience." He states that such people are more performance oriented than communication oriented.

Communication-oriented individuals focus on telling their story, expressing their opinions, and presenting information. They view public speaking in the same way they view having everyday conversations with other people. Performance-oriented individuals, on the other hand, view public speaking as an activity that requires special skills. They also view the audience not as listeners but as judges who are there only to evaluate the individual's performance as a speaker. And this is where the problem lies, because, according to Tsaousides, "when the focus shifts from being heard and understood to being evaluated, the anxiety tends to be higher."

However, there is an important fact we must note: thoughts are birthed by knowledge and information. And there are certain conditions that inform and shape a person's thoughts towards developing a phobia for public speaking.

Why people fear public speaking #4: Conditions

"It is not a person or situation that affects your life; it is the meaning you give to that person or situation, which influences your emotions and actions. Your choice is to change the meaning you gave it or to change your response, in order to create the outcome you want."

SHANNON L. ALDER

There are people who dread electrical or electronic appliances, not because they've suffered an electrical shock themselves, but perhaps because they witnessed someone killed or maimed as a result. Certain situations or events can create a perpetual fear in a person. These events may have happened to the person directly or they witnessed it happening to someone else.

Many people are afraid of public speaking because of events they have witnessed. These events shape their thoughts and orient their minds towards viewing public speaking as a difficult activity. Some of the conditions or events that could predispose a person to glossophobia include:

- *A poor public speaking performance in the past*: If an individual at some point had an unsuccessful public speaking experience in all likelihood that person may never want to try public speaking again. He will always remember and revisit that event where he stammered all through with a shaky voice, and where the audience was amused by his anxiety—and he will be forever scarred by it.

- *Watching someone else perform poorly at public speaking*: This can create an impression and misperception in the mind of the individual that public speaking is difficult.

- *Negative reactions from the audience*: There are audiences that aren't receptive to the public speaker or to the message being put forth. They are either inattentive to the speaker or, in extreme cases, boo the speaker off the stage. During an Iraqi press conference in December 2008, an Iraqi journalist famously hurled both of his shoes at the then president of the United States, George W. Bush. Such a scenario passes on the subtle message that public speaking can be a risky, if not dangerous engagement where one is vulnerable and can be attacked should they not win the favor of their audience.And, we can add this this message to the list of "what ifs" associated with glossophobia.

Theo Tsaousides compiles a list of other conditions that can make a person more anxious about public speaking. They are:

- *Inexperience*: The freelance writer I mentioned earlier was afraid to take up big gigs because he thought he wasn't experienced enough or skilled enough to handle such tasks. The same thing plays out in a glossophobic person. If the individual feels they lack experience in public speaking, it only serves to heighten their fear of speaking in public.

- *Evaluation*: Tsaousides notes that a real or imagined evaluation heightens the fear of public speaking. A person who feels that the audience will assess his public speaking performance may become too afraid and unwilling to speak.

- *Status difference*: A glossophobic person may not have issues speaking to high school students—but what happens when the person is required to speak at an event where the governor of a state would be present? Anyone, I am sure would be nervous about this, even people who don't suffer from glossophobia. Some staff of corporate organizations who are called upon to present a pitch before the board of directors or top professionals in the industry come to experience this a lot. As a matter of fact, their fear is two-fold: their fear of speaking before people higher than them, and their fear of being evaluated by these people.
- *New ideas*: There is a reluctance and an uncertainty that usually accompanies charting a new territory. Any person

who is required to speak will definitely be more comfortable speaking on a subject they are familiar with, as opposed to a subject they are not familiar with. As a matter of fact, I routinely advise people to speak on subjects that they have interest in. This is one of the secrets of top public speakers. However, there are cases where a person may be required to speak on an entirely new topic that reaches well beyond their realm of understanding. In such cases, this where we may see fear set in. Tsaousides writes that, "When your public appearance involves presenting something new, quite often you may feel more uncomfortable stating your position, taking questions from the audience, or dealing with those audience members who try to poke holes."

- *New audience*: Speaking to a familiar audience often poses no problem. However, when one is required to speak before a new audience, fear sets in. (It is similar to what happens when one is required to speak before people who have higher status or rank.) The person begins to wonder if the audience will like them, whether they communicate effectively, if the audience will understand them, if their thoughts are clear enough, if they possess the skills required to deliver the speech convincingly, and well.

Why people fear public speaking #5: Skills

"Without sharpening your weapon, standing on the battlefield would not increase your chance of winning."

ANKIT SAHAY

"Everyone can be doing the same thing but what will make you stand out is your level of skill. Many have attributed success to opportunity. True, opportunity is a key factor for success. However, an opportunity that doesn't meet a skill when it comes will not result in success."

RON MALHOTRA

A person who feels they lack basic public speaking skills will be scared of public speaking. Skills beget confidence. In the consistent debate about who the better player is between Cristiano Ronaldo and Lionel Messi, I have come to realize that one major reason why the fans love Ronaldo more is because he invests time and money to sharpen his skill. Many of his fans know that he is not as talented as his Argentine rival, but they appreciate the level of hard work and sheer dedication he has built into his skill. Ronaldo understands that he must be a hard worker and build his skills, and this is why he speaks with so much confidence, a confidence often mistaken for arrogance.

As one improves in an endeavor, one becomes more

enthusiastic to take up bigger tasks. An important fact to note: when you are not doing enough to invest and grow your skill, you will also know. You can lie to everyone but yourself. Knowing that you have not committed yourself properly, not spent the time, money and energy to grow your skill contributes greatly to your fear of public speaking. The old adage, 'fake it till you make it,' therefore, does not ring true; one must build their skill up slowly and steadily upon solid foundations for it to have a lasting impact.

Theo Tsaousides quips: "The people who work on their skills instead of relying on natural talent are the speakers who stand out the most." This means that sharpening your skill is one of the key secrets to handling and overcoming your fear of public speaking.

Overcoming Glossophobia

"It is not the critic who counts; not the man who points out how the strong man stumbles, or where the doer of deeds could have done them better. The credit belongs to the man who is actually in the arena, whose face is marred by dust and sweat and blood; who strives valiantly; who errs, who comes up short again and again, because there is no effort without error and shortcoming; but who does actually strive to do the deeds; who knows great enthusiasms, the great devotions; who spends himself in a worthy cause; who at the best knows in the end the triumph of high achievement, and who at the worst, if he fails, at least fails while daring greatly, so that his place shall never be with those cold and timid souls who neither know victory nor defeat."

THEODORE ROOSEVELT

The words of Theodore Roosevelt summarize what it takes to overcome any fear. This includes glossophobia. With these words I could easily proceed to the next section of this book. However, since we have just looked at the five top reasons why people fear public speaking, I feel it important to address how to overcome these fears.

Overcoming Glossophobia #1: Physiology

"The credit belongs to the man who is actually in the arena, whose face is marred by dust and sweat and blood…"

Glossophobia is classified as a social anxiety disorder (SAD) that can be managed with drugs and other forms of therapy. Pharmacological therapies include the use of short-term drugs classed as beta-blockers which block the symptoms of anxiety. Non-pharmacological management includes short-term therapies like systematic desensitization and cognitive-behavioral therapy (Arlin Cuncic, 2020).

Systematic desensitization is a technique developed by Joseph Wolpe, a pioneer of behavioral therapy, that is a based on the *principles of classical conditioning* (a learning process that occurs through interactions between environmental and naturally occurring stimuli) *and* the *assumption* that what has been learned can be unlearned (Sheryl Ankrom, 2020; Kendra Cherry, 2019). On the other hand, Cognitive-behavioral therapy (CBT) is often a combination of different techniques used to *identify* an individual's irrational beliefs and thought patterns, *replacing* them with more realistic ones (Arlin Cuncic, 2020).

If the glossophobic individual feels that they cannot handle their glossophobia, a doctor or therapist can guide them through these pharmacological or non-pharmacological therapies. However, I believe that a glossophobic person can overcome their fear without drugs or other forms of therapies. In fact, therapies like CBT use techniques that an individual can practice on their own. All it requires is focus and intentionality. It requires choosing courage as a habit.

Overcoming Glossophobia #2:
Deal with Low Self-esteem

"It is not the critic who counts; not the man
who points out how the strong man stumbles…"

Self-worth is the intrinsic value of a person. Low self-esteem isn't the absence of self-worth, it is the blindness to this worth. And this blindness occurs when we measure our value using others as a yardstick. This shouldn't be so. *Life* is the only yardstick that should be used to measure our value. As long as we are living beings we have worth and we are worthy. Keep reminding yourself of this truth, no matter what might have triggered your feelings of low self-esteem.

It may be you had or have disapproving or uninvolved authority figures who never commend your achievements. It's probably heartbreaking, but it shouldn't dampen your feeling of self-worth. You are an achiever. Commendations or criticisms do not take away this fact. If you have excelled in one area before, you can also excel at public speaking. This should be your motivation. Your excellence is not tied to the praises or validation of authority figures in your life. For instance, if you had good grades in school yet received disapproving remarks from parents or guardians, does it change the fact that you made good grades? Your results should be your first encouragement. Praise from people should only be viewed as icing on the cake. So do not fear public speaking because of past disapprovals. Always look back to your achievements. They are your validations, your proof of work. If you could do it then, you can do it now.

If you have been bullied, do not see yourself as the loser. You are not the problem. The bully is. As a matter of fact, bullies are disturbed individuals with low self-esteem who depend on harassing others to feel good about themselves. When you allow them get to you, you let them win, you show them that they are powerful enough to change you. Do not let this happen. Stand up to them. Keep winning. Show them they failed at getting under your skin. Get on stage. Speak with confidence. Understand that you have value to offer. And if for any reason, your audience attempts to bully you, walk away with your head high. It is their loss, not yours. They've only deprived themselves of the value they could have received. The bully is trying to make you alter the narrative about yourself. Never hand them the pen. It's yours for keeps. Write what you want, and not what they want you to write.

If you are still disturbed about your past, let it go. True, you may have done things you aren't proud of, but that doesn't mean you should hide your head in shame forever. Who knows whether you had to go through those past events so you could have the story to share with others today, and show them a better way? So, why run away from speaking in public when the world is waiting to hear your story, when the lives of many depend on your story? This reminds me of Muniba Mazari Baloch, a 33-year old Pakistani activist and motivational speaker. I listened to her speech titled, "We All Are Perfectly Imperfect," which she delivered at TEDx Islamabad in 2014, and I was completely awed by her grit.

Rolling her wheelchair on stage and looking at the crowd that filled the coliseum, she told her story—the story of her failed marriage, and a marriage that resulted in the loss of her mobility.. It was the story of how her deep need to seek out her father's approval, please her father in her younger years had shaped her to the point where, instead of following her dream of becoming a painter, she became the housewife of a selfish man who one day carelessly fell asleep while they were out driving; when the car fell into a ditch, he jumped out and saved himself, leaving her to her own sad fate. This singular event changed her life forever. At the end of her talk, Muniba said that her "perfectly imperfect life made her who and what she is today."

But what if Muniba had wallowed in self-pity and regret? What if she had held on to her past and refused to share her story? How would other women be able to learn through her not to give up on their dreams for a second rate marriage? How would parents understand that there are times they should just allow their children to do what make them happy, rather than being constantly on the path of seeking approval? And, how would other men understand the importance of love and sacrifice; understand that they shouldn't marry those they don't care about? How would people learn not to be defined and held back by adversity? As we can see, the lessons to be learned from this speech are not only potentially life changing, but far-reaching. In the beginning of the speech, Muniba made this profound statement: "I believe in the power of words. Many people speak before they think. But I know the value of words. Words can make you or break you, they can heal your soul, they can damage you forever. So I always try to use positive words in my life wherever I go. They call it adversity; I call it opportunity. They call it weakness; I call it strength. They call me disabled, I call myself "differently abled." They see my disability. I see my ability."

You too can borrow a leaf from Muniba's book. Her experiences came at a great cost, yet Muniba did not dwell in it; she used what she had learned to be the light and empower and educate others. Shape your life with your words, not by your past. Shape your life by giving your mind a new orientation.

Finally, don't be triggered by the media. Don't be moved by the glamour seen around social media. Live your life on your terms. When you watch top public speakers they should inspire you, not make you afraid. Aspire to speak like them. Understand that the expertise you see behind the stage wasn't acquired in a day. So aim to learn. Don't be intimidated. Imitation is a part of learning. Imitate the speakers you admire.

Use their methods to practice. As you do this, you will notice that you begin to develop your own style and technique. But it all starts with learning from the best and by not being intimidated by them.

Overcoming Glossophobia #3:
Reform your thoughts

"…who at the best knows in the end the triumph of high achievement, and who at the worst, if he fails, at least fails while daring greatly…"

Sometimes, we close our minds to things we haven't even attempted. How do you know you'd be a bad public speaker when you haven't even tried public speaking before? Alright, let's assume that you've tried before and performed poorly—is that enough reason to shut your mind against it? If a child tries to walk and stumbles and falls, and because of this decides that he will never try to walk again, the world would be filled with crawling men and women.

Reform your thoughts. Think about your ability. Never dampen the can-do spirit in you. Do away with all the negatives in your head—"I cannot be a good speaker," "I may come off as boring," "I am scared of crowds," "I will stutter." Just like Munabi, replace these negatives with the positives. The words we speak are first produced in our minds. So choose to say—"I have what it takes to be a good speaker," "I am lively. My audience cannot be bored when I'm speaking," "I am not scared of crowds. They are people just like me. People are just waiting to listen to me speak," "I will speak eloquently and coherently." When you reform your thoughts, your words and actions are reformed too. It won't be long before you start acting according to your thoughts and beliefs.

Another reason why your thoughts are influenced negatively towards public speaking is because you are worried about the audience's perception of you. There is no need to be afraid of public speaking because you are worried about how others will look at you. Funnily enough, the truth is that other people have their own problems to think about, and are more likely to be dwelling on their own insecurities, not yours—so why do you think they care about you? The audience are there to listen to you, to receive value, and then take that value back to their own lives. Why else do they come to listen to you, if not to learn something?

It is not erroneous to say that pride plays an important role in this. I know it is probably ironic, but it is not far-fetched. People who are afraid of public speaking because they are more concerned about the perceptions they think others have about them consider themselves *too* important that they think that others notice and judge them, even when this is not the case.

So, focus instead on communicating, not performing. Share your story in the same way you would tell it to a friend. When you focus on being heard and understood, the performance required to deliver the speech will come naturally to you. But when you are more performance-centered and thinking only about the audience's perception of you, you won't perform well enough. Funnily enough, this belief is valid and one hundred percent true. This is what I mean. Let's imagine you are to speak to an audience of a hundred people. In the audience, you have those who love the rhythmical eloquence of Barack Obama; those who are intrigued by the audacious, sometimes cussing tone of Gary Vaynerchuk; those who are excited by Steve

Rizzo's humor; those who have one public speaking preference or the other. So how would you please these people, given their range of diverse preferences with your own performance? This is the trouble with being performance-centered. You cannot possibly entertain everyone or meet everyone's expectations—so, rather than worry about their perceptions of you, and just "do" you.

People may likely forget a performance, but words stay forever in the mind. Concentrate on effectively using your words to communicate; reach out and touch your audience, access the deepest recesses of the mind to enlighten, to educate, to show the audience something they have never thought about.

Overcoming Glossophobia #4: Refuse to be conditioned by events

"...who errs, who comes up short again and again, because there is no effort without error and shortcoming; but who does actually strive to do the deeds..."

I try as much as possible not to be conditioned by

events, whether positive or negative. I believe that we are to learn and come out stronger when something happens to us. We shouldn't alter our personality or put aside what we love because of a situation. I read the story of a chef who attributed his cooking skill and confidence to his mom. He said that he had always loved to cook as a child. He was fifteen when his elder sister brought her fiancé to come see the family. His mom let him take charge of the cooking that day. However, he got distracted and the food turned out salty. His mom came into the kitchen, tasted the food and told him that everyone would just have to eat the meal that way. She apologized to their guest, and the whole family ate the meal with joy, despite that fact of his being flushed with embarrassment. But what surprised him more was that they were to receive another guest a week later, and his mom didn't hesitate to put him in charge of the cooking again. He didn't want to do it and he reminded her of the last experience. She smiled and answered, "No one has ever achieved anything great by hiding behind shame and embarrassment. No event is totally bad, because there is always a lesson in every event. And lessons make us better."

So this same message I bring to you: there is no event bad enough that should ever make you avoid public speaking. Always find the positives in everything.

A poor public speaking performance in the past does not mean you will always perform poorly. Go back to the drawing board. Find out where you got it wrong and work on your next performance. No one ever told you that you would get it right with your first performance. Even professional public speakers have bad days sometimes. But one bad day is insignificant compared to the countless good days.

Watching someone perform poorly at public speaking doesn't translate to you performing poorly yourself. I have heard people say that you become what you behold. This is true. But what they don't let you know is that what you behold must first take root in your mind before you become it. So do not let the failure of another stop you from becoming who you want to be. Do not let their failure take root in your mind. A peculiar trait about human beings is our herd mentality. Most of the things we do we learnt from watching and imitating others. But it is out of place to allow the herd mentality to make you think you are a failure. You are unique. You can conquer ground where others have failed. That your friend failed a course doesn't mean that you will fail. That your parents failed at marriage doesn't mean yours won't be successful. In the same vein, just because someone had a poor public speaking performance doesn't mean you'll perform poorly, too.

In life, there will be people who will adore you and those who will dislike you. Never let condemnation stop you from being who you want to be. Negative reactions from an audience shouldn't stop you from being a public speaker. Learn from footballers: there are times when the fans boo them and criticize them, but you still see them playing in the next match. This is what public speaking should be like Deafen your ears to the criticisms of the audience. Meeting a toxic audience may be part of your public speaking journey, but it shouldn't be the end of the journey. Lock it up in your bag of experiences and move on.

Also, do not let inexperience deter you from speaking. Nobody was born a master. Even child prodigies have to be educated. Being inexperienced is not a flaw; it is remaining inexperienced that becomes the problem. If you are inexperienced as a public speaker, work hard to perfect your craft. Never be limited by fear. If you decide not to speak because of inexperience, how will you ever get the experience you seek? The greatest footballer had a debut match. The Oscar winning actor had a debut film. The Grammy award winner had a debut single. The Pulitzer Prize winner for literature had a debut novel. Greatness isn't a tree that emerges out of nothing, it is a seed that blossoms. Never be afraid to speak. Just start, just speak.

Audience evaluation should not make you scared of speaking. It shouldn't even be a problem in the first place if you are more communication-centered than performance-centered. So focus on communicating effectively, and the audience will love you. This also applies when you are speaking to a new audience or to people with higher status than you. Yes, they might be more knowledgeable than you, but there is a reason why you were asked to speak. So let that reason be your source of strength and courage.

Finally, I understand how speaking on a new idea can be unnerving. But expel the anxiety by carrying out a great deal of research. A ghostwriter once told me that he was asked to write a book on the stock options market and that the book must read like it was written by someone in that niche. He almost turned down the job. But what did he do? He used a week to watch videos and read countless articles on stock options. By the time he completed the book he was so knowledgeable he could comfortably hold a class on the subject. So when you are required to speak on a new subject, carry out your research. Ask questions. Compare narratives. Make sure you arm yourself with as much knowledge as you can find. It is often said that knowledge is power. Let me to add that: knowledge is also courage.

Overcoming Glossophobia #5: Develop your skill

"…who does actually strive to do the deeds; who knows great enthusiasms, the great devotions; who spends himself in a worthy cause…"

Build self confidence by developing yourself. I have had people tell me that they are scared of public speaking. So I start a conversation with them by asking them a series of questions:

— How many books have you read this year?

— Two

— We've spent more than half of the year already, and you've read only two books?

— Yes

— Alright. Let me assume that you are busy. How many articles have you read across top magazines and newspapers like *The Guardian*, *New York Times*, *Granta*, *The Economist*, *Washington Post*, *Wall Street Journal*, and so on?

— None. Or, let's say one or two trending news articles that I am interested in.

— Wow! OK. How many public speaking videos have you watched so far?

— Only a few.

— What about books or articles on public speaking?

— Just few, too.

— Have you attended a free or premium class on public speaking?

— Not many.

— OK...what about learning from YouTube videos?

— That has never crossed my mind.

I am usually dumbfounded and exhausted after the conversation. It is unfortunate to see people claim to love an art but do not do anything to improve themselves. Yet, they wonder why they are afraid to speak. As a matter of fact, their fear is valid. As I mentioned earlier, we can lie to everyone but ourselves. Their fear of public speaking is birthed from the knowledge that they are not working hard enough. They are scared of being disgraced by their incompetence, and deep down they know they could have done more to educate themselves.

So examine yourself. Why are you scared of public speaking? Is it because you know you are not developing your skill? If this is the case, retrace your steps and start developing yourself.

Read books to develop your grammar and broaden

your insights.

Also read books on rhetoric, oratory and public speaking to learn the necessary skills that you need.

Watch top public speakers and take note of their style.

Practice what you have learned when you are alone. You can watch yourself in the mirror and take note of your gestures and facial expressions.

Finally, do not shy away from speaking before an audience. Speaking before an audience is the only way to test the effectiveness of what you have learned.

Famous people who suffered glossophobia

"I think this is what we all want to hear: that we are not alone in hitting the bottom, and that it is possible to come out of that place courageous, beautiful, and strong."

ANNA WHITE

As human beings, we often feel that what we go through is entirely specific to us. We feel that others have never been in our shoes, so they wouldn't understand our worry, complaints, or fear. But this is not true. For everything you've gone through, there have been others who have also gone through the same. Some overcame, others did not. But the fact remains that whatever you have experienced in your life is not specifically just to you. This is why I think it's important to now show you some famous people who have also suffered glossophobia.

When you are famous, you're required to speak to a large audience from time to time. For us to know these famous individuals means that they did not allow themselves to be limited by their fears. We've heard them speak or read transcripts of their speeches. But little did we know that they were once glossophobic. You will probably be shocked by some of the names I list here, because their words have inspired and encouraged many. A feat which wouldn't have been possible if they had hidden themselves behind the curtain of glossophobia. So here is a list of famous people who were once scared of public speaking.

This list has been compiled from a variety of different sources.

Mahatma Gandhi

"There would be nothing to frighten if you refused to be afraid."

It would be difficult for one to believe that, at one time the great Indian revolutionist and leader could not string two words together in public. As a student, he suffered frequent panic attacks anytime he was to face the crowd. He recalled a particular experience where he was supposed to speak to a vegetarian community in London. Gripped with anxiety, he could only read one line from the speech he had prepared and had to ask someone to help him read the rest. Narrating the agonizing experience years later, he said, "My vision became blurred and I trembled, though the speech hardly covered a sheet of foolscap."

It took so long for Gandhi to conquer his battle with glossophobia. Scott Stossel writing in a 2014 issue of *The Atlantic* stated that, "What Gandhi called 'the awful strain of public speaking' prevented him for years from speaking up . . . and nearly deterred him from developing into the spiritual leader he ultimately became." At one point he even steered clear of speaking at dinner parties and friendly get-togethers. But it is also ironic that a glossophobic person would decide to be a lawyer. During Gandhi's first case before a judge, he panicked and left the courtroom. It was a humiliating experience. Recalling the experience, Ghandi wrote: "My head was reeling and I felt as though the whole court was doing likewise. I could think of no question to ask."

But how did Mahatma Gandhi overcome his fear of public speaking and make his voice heard around the globe? The answer: passion. Nayomi Chibana put it accurately when she wrote, "Gandhi found a cause that inflamed a passion so great in him that it overrode his anxieties and fears." Motivated by his desire to see India freed, he defeated his fears and spoke up for what he believed in. Also, Gandhi's life confirms what I stated earlier about how finding the positives in every situation, whether good or bad, helps us overcome fear. According to Chibana, Gandhi later saw his "hesitancy in speech" as an advantage, saying that it taught him to pack meaning into short but powerful statements.

Thomas Jefferson

"Nothing can stop the man with the right mental attitude from achieving his goal; nothing on earth can help the man with the wrong mental attitude."

The third president of the United States of America. Founding Father of America. Defender of democracy. Primary author of the Declaration of Independence. Glossophobic.

Thomas Jefferson's glossophobia was an even more pathetic case than Mahatma Gandhi's. Stossel reveals that Jefferson's law career was cut short because of his fear of public speaking. (But I digress: what is this strong connection between glossophobic individuals and law?) Stossel further records that Jefferson never spoke during deliberations of the Second Continental Congress. John Adams, a fellow congressman and Jefferson's predecessor, commented on Jefferson's fear in his autobiography, *Diary and Autobiography of John Adams*. Adams wrote: "Mr. Jefferson had been now for about a year a Member of Congress, but had attended his Duty in the House but a very small part of the time and when there had never spoken in public; and during the whole time I sat (*sic*) with him in Congress, I never heard him utter three sentences together. The most of a speech he ever made in my hearing was a gross insult on Religion, in one or two sentences, for which I gave him immediately the Reprehension, which he richly merited."

Furthermore, Jefferson's inaugural addresses were the only two speeches he gave during his time as President. Chibana writes that those present at these speeches said Jefferson spoke in such a low tone that they could barely hear him. Another biographer of Jefferson notes that if Jefferson attempted to speak loudly, "his voice would sink in his throat."

According to Stossel, psychiatrists at Duke University, after reviewing presidential biographies and other materials, diagnosed Jefferson posthumously of social phobia. This diagnosis was documented in *The Journal of Nervous and Mental Disease.*

Not much is known about how Jefferson handled his glossophobia. Chibana states that he worked around his fear by relying on his writing abilities. However, aside from his writing abilities, I would like to believe that Jefferson never allowed his fear of public speaking to hold him back. It is true he spoke only when necessary, but he didn't let fear make him choose not to speak at all.

Winston Churchill

"Fear is a reaction. Courage is a decision."

We remember Winston Churchill as the British prime minister who led Britain successfully through the Second World War. We also remember him for his doggedness and inspiring speeches. We remember him for these things though interestingly enough, we no longer remember that once had a fear of public speaking.

Winston grew up with a lisp and this caused him to have a lifelong struggle with public speaking. He often memorized his speeches word for word and spoke without any notes. However, just like Gandhi, Churchill once had a humiliating public speaking experience. At just 29 with a budding political career ahead of him, Churchill was required to give a speech before the House of Commons. In his usual manner, he spoke without any notes until he lost his train of thought.

Narrating the story in their article, "The Winston Churchill Guide to Public Speaking," Brett & Kate McKay write: "'And it rests with those who. . .' Churchill begins to say. But he trails off, losing his train of thought. 'It rests with those who. . .' he repeats again, yet famouslyfails to finish the sentence, or pivot to another topic. For three long, agonizing minutes, Churchill gropes desperately for his next line and cannot for the life of him retrieve it. The House heckles him. His face turns red. Finally he sits down, putting his head in his hands in utter dejection."

Churchill's experience is a perfect example of how certain situations can instil the fear of death in a person when trying to make a public speech. This singular experience was capable of turning Churchill into a mute, never to speak before a crowd again. Thankfully, this never happened. Churchill learnt from his mistake. After that event, he vowed to memorize his speeches as he had always done, but this time he would be on stage with his notes. Commenting on this new technique, Brett & Kate write, "Improvising is truly a manly art, but so is admitting a weakness. Churchill had the humility to recognize that he didn't have the knack for extemporaneous speaking. So he worked around it, so much so, that most listeners didn't even realize that he was reading from notes."

Kris Deichler notes that, in order to get his speeches right, Churchill often spent hours planning and practicing his words, perfecting every minute of what he would say. Winston Churchill's strategy for defeating the demons of glossophobia could be adapted and turned into a complete guide on how to overcome the fear of public speaking as coming from one of the world's greatest leaders. We will examine these excellent strategies later on.

Harrison Ford

"Work hard and figure out how to be useful and don't try to imitate anybody else's success. Figure out how to do it for yourself, with yourself."

A headline on *Metro* reads: "Julia Roberts and Harrison Ford lead a long list of celebs who have conquered public speaking fear."

From Han Solo to Indiana Jones to President James Marshall. Who would have thought that the handsome, brilliant actor, Harrison Ford, once feared public speaking? He may look fearless in his movies, but Eileen Bailey notes that the actor has previously admitted to being scared of people.

In 2000, when he was honored by the American Film Institute with a Life Achievement Award, Mr. Ford struggled with his acceptance speech. To this, he later admitted to the *Los Angeles Times* that his greatest fear is public speaking. According to Bailey, he said he also experienced this fear when any of his characters were required to make a speech. For Ford, public speaking was "a mixed bag of terror and anxiety."

But he didn't accept his glossophobia as a situation he couldn't work on. According to Stephanie Sparer, Harrison Ford learned to practice public speaking consistently. He put his energies into speaking and delivering his lines slowly and with confidence. And it worked.

Julia Roberts

"Wit is the key, I think to anybody's heart, because who doesn't like to laugh?"

For me, Julia Roberts comes across as a spirited woman. She once said, "When I have a choice between normality and insanity, I choose insanity." So it was difficult for me to reconcile the lively 52-year-old with glossophobia. Unbelievable as it may sound, Roberts once feared public speaking. And the major reason for this was because she stuttered a lot as a child.

Ironically, in *Larry Crowne*, a 2011 romantic comedy film, Julia played the role of not just a college professor, but a professor of public speaking. Amol Sarva, a *Huffpost* contributor, writes that Julia confessed that she was terrified of the teaching scenes. About those scenes, Julia said, "All these faces looking up at me, thinking, What is she going to teach us? I needed to find my composure. It was very hard—it was terrible, in fact."

Sarva further notes that Julia is often not vocal about her stuttering and public speaking struggles, however she once confided that she overcame her stuttering and achieved fluid speech through speech therapy, which boosted her public speaking confidence. She also expressed interest in being a spokesperson for the Stuttering Foundation of America, a nonprofit organization that provides support to those who stutter, and and also supports research into the causes of stuttering.

What I have tried to do so far here is to show the practical applications on how to overcome the fear of public speaking by dissolving the myths that surround it. And that, by applying the methods I've previously outlined, even celebrity identities have managed to hurdle and conquer the mountain of fear that lies behind glossophobia. . Julia subscribed to a physiological method of therapy and it worked for her. Also, in remarking about Julia's win over glossophobia, Sarva corroborates my earlier words when he writes, "Roberts is a remarkable example of endeavoring to persevere. She sought the help she needed, and overcame with incredible tenacity." Then he goes further to ask: "What is that thing we want? Are we letting fear dictate our action (or inaction)? What if Julia Roberts had thought to herself, *'I'm just not very good at public speaking, and this stutter will never go away. Acting just isn't for me?"* It's powerful food for thought.

Rowan Atkinson

"People think because I can make them laugh on the stage, I'll be able to make them laugh in person. That isn't the case at all. I am essentially a rather quiet, dull person who just happens to be a performer."

Of all the famous people who have suffered from glossophobia, Rowan Atkinson (aka Mr. Bean) doesn't actually come as a surprise to me. I have watched a couple of his interviews, and, for a comedian, I find him strangely reserved when he is off stage. Some of his statements about his personality and/or the Mr. Bean character also point to this fact; for example, in the quote above, Rowan considers himself a rather dull and ordinary person. He has also made statements like: "But generally speaking, I tend to be quiet and introspective." "Mr. Bean is at his best when he is not using words, but I am equally at home in both verbal and nonverbal expression." "Funny things tend not to happen to me. I am not a natural comic. I need to think about things a lot before I can be even remotely amusing."

Cátia Isabel Silva states that Atkinson gets very nervous and uncomfortable when he has to speak in public—a trait that is easily spotted when he is at talk shows. Part of Atkinson's coping mechanism, Silva notes, was his ability to blend characters showing problems with speech as a way of masking his own struggles. The most popular of his characters, Mr. Bean, is an almost silent comedy show.

But like Gandhi and Roberts, Atkinson would not allow himself to be limited by fear when there is a greater need to speak. Silva recalls that the comedian stepped forward in 2012 when he needed to defend what he believed was correct: he pushed his evident discomfort aside and "made a heartfelt statement about freedom of speech."

Richard Branson

"Whatever your goal is, you will never succeed unless you let go of your fears and fly."

Of Richard Branson, Jenny Medeiros writes: "It's hard to believe that someone who is constantly pitching ideas, meeting with investors, and giving interviews would detest speaking in public, but it's true." Branson himself is quoted to have said, "I loathe making speeches, and always have." Funnily enough, he is one of the world's highest paid speakers. In a 2016 report, *Inc.* states that Branson receives in excess of $100,000 for every public speaking engagement.

Although he dislikes public speaking, Branson has taken deliberate steps to work on his fear and weaknesses. In her article for *Goalcast*, Medeiros reveals Branson's bulletproof strategy for overcoming his glossophobia. First of all, Branson imagines that speaking to an audience is like having a chat with a friend in his living room. Buttressing this point, Medeiros writes, ". . . every time Branson is tasked with public speaking, he ignores the fact there are millions of people watching him. Instead, he casually sits on stage and pretends he's telling a story to a group of friends." Secondly, being motivated by the words of Mark Twain, the billionaire never fails to prepare his speeches. Mark Twain said: "Impromptu speaking— that is a difficult thing. I used to begin about a week ahead, and write out my impromptu speech and get it by heart."

Thirdly, as simple as it may sound, Branson relies on practice. He takes a cue from the life of Winston Churchill, whom he said practised an hour for every minute of his speech.

Richard Branson understood the importance of overcoming one's fears and found ways to quiet and deaden his fear. Now he is one of the highest paid public speakers in the world. This just goes to show that there is always a reward on the other side of fear.

Samuel L. Jackson

"If you do not have courage, you may not have the opportunity to use any of your other virtues."

What comes to your mind when you see Samuel L. Jackson on your screen? Hardcore. Intense. Tough.

You would also remember him by the number of times he uses the MF cuss word. And there is a reason why he uses this word that rhymes with "mother hawker" excessively. Like Julia Roberts, Samuel stutters and suffers from a speaking phobia.

Toastmasters International, a nonprofit educational organization that teaches public speaking, states that Samuel heeded the advice of his speech therapist who recommended he take up acting as a way to help him overcome his stutter and phobia. Acting helped, but it was the "MF" word that helped more. Abigail Gillibrand in her *Metro* article reveals that the actor explained, in a chat on The Howard Stern Show, how the word helped stop his stutter. Samuel said, "I have no idea how, but it just does. It flicks a switch that stops the d-d-d-b-b-b, because I stuttered really, really, really badly for a long time."

Jackson's method for overcoming glossophobia shows us that there are cases when one should seek out therapy. Using a cuss word to stop stuttering and overcome a speaking phobia may sound strange, but it is a brilliant technique that has worked—and is working—for the award winning actor. I think when it comes to defeating glossophobia, the end always justifies the means.

Abraham Lincoln

"You can have anything you want if you want it badly enough. You can be anything you want to be, do anything you set out to accomplish if you hold to that desire with singleness of purpose."

There is a story of a man, a US congressman and lawyer who wasn't so popular outside his home state of Illinois. But one day, he managed to attract a sizeable audience of about 1,500 people and he spoke to them at the Cooper Union Hall in New York City. He spoke against slavery with eloquent delivery. It was a powerful speech, one that resonated with the people so much that they nominated him for President of the United States, a position he would later go on to win. But something funny happened: after his rousing address in New York City, he was invited to speak in New Jersey a month later, but he declined. Why? He got nervous and too was scared to speak in public.

This is the story of the 16th President of the United States of America, Abraham Lincoln. When he was invited by the Republican committee to speak in New Jersey, Lincoln sent them a short and curt note that read: "I cannot speak in New Jersey this time. I have overstayed my time — have heard something about sickness in my family — and really am nervous and unfit to fill my engagement already made here in Connecticut. Will you please excuse me?"

Nayomi Chibana states that the note itself revealed that "Lincoln was not comfortable with his increasing notoriety and was anxious to the point of missing out on an important opportunity." Gary Genard similarly wrote that Lincoln's refusal to speak at New Jersey was a classic symptom of speech anxiety, "the combination of visibility and vulnerability."

But Lincoln soldiered ahead to overcome this fear. Unlike Thomas Jefferson, who gave only two speeches during his entire eight year tenure as President, Lincoln gave many speeches in his four year reign. Over the years, Lincoln has become well known for his oratory and speeches. As a matter of fact, many have dissected his speeches to discover what made them such powerful and unique deliveries. Just like Churchill, Lincoln provides us with a solid template for effective public speaking, and we will look into this later.

King George VI

"A sick King is no good to anyone. There must be no weakness. No vulnerability. [And so I will speak] because I have a right to be heard. I have a voice!"

Even royalty was not immune to glossophobia. King George VI is famously remembered for his nervous stutter and difficult speeches. After King Edward abdicated the throne in 1936 (running off with his American love, Wallis Simpson), little brother King George VI was unexpectedly thrust into the limelight, assuming the great seat of power, and along with it, his addresses to the nation. England was heading into WWII, and the pressure was on the King to navigate rough waters and lead his country through tough times. It is said he engaged the help of everyone from speech therapists to experts to help him get through his speeches. In his daily speech therapy, King George would play loud music as he practiced his readings aloud so that he would not be able to hear himself speak, thus overcoming the crippling nervousness that so plagued him. A lifelong stutterer unwittingly thrown onto the throne, it was George's famous speech in 1939, when announcing that England was going to war against Germany, that he won the hearts and minds of his people. The King used a physical copy of the address from which to read, highlighting places where he should consider pausing, or swapping words out for something easier to pronounce. And it paid off — the King delivered the speech beautifully, now considered one of his most iconic addresses. In 2010, Hollywood would produce the film adaptation, The King's Speech, showcasing his lifelong struggle with public speaking.

Adele

*"I'm ballsy. I have guts. I'm not afraid of anyone.
I think that's what makes me feel powerful."*

The "Hello" crooner is the contemporary poster child who is proof that anyone can   develop glossophobia as a result of being in the public eye. A *Forbes* article by Carmine Gallo reveals that the British singer suffers from severe stage fright because she cares so much about her fans, worries about their perceptions of her, and doesn't want to let them down. Gallo wrote a short transcript of an interview Adele had with Matt Lauer, where she confessed to how nervous she was before one of concerts, promoted as, "Live in New York City."

Adele: "I saw the crowd and I just melted. After the second or third song, I was chill, I was alright."

Lauer: "What are you like when you get nervous?"

Adele: "I get fidgety, I moan, I complain, I try to escape, I try to get out."

In another interview, Adele made a statement highlighting the negative impacts of fear. She said, "I get so nervous with live performances that I'm too frightened to try anything new."

But Adele learnt—and is learning—to face her fears. According to Gallo, she apparently was quoted as saying, "We can't manage fear if we don't face our fears." When she started out as a singer, Adele said she preferred to perform in smaller, low-key venues as a way of coping with her nervousness. But the singer has gone ahead to perform at the 02 arena in London which has a seating capacity of 20,000. She has also performed at Madison Square Garden which seats 20,000 people, The Staples Center, which seats about 13,000 people, the Glastonbury Festival with over 200,000 people in attendance, and the 82,500-seater ANZ Stadium in Sydney. For someone with glossophobia and performance anxiety, she has done well for herself. Gallo—who notes that psychotherapists recommend that people manage their fear by exposing themselves to the fear repeatedly—likens Adele's performance fears before large audiences as akin to someone who stands before a tarantula and suffers from arachnophobia.

When I stumbled upon Adele's quote, I had to wonder if it wasn't ironic for someone with performance anxiety to refer to herself as "ballsy" and as someone who has guts. But it is not ironic. Words are powerful. I would like to believe that Adele's telling herself those words and *believing* them played a major role in her shifting her away from fear .

As I said before, always find the positives in everything. Carmine Gallo followed this line of thought when he gave an advice to those who suffer stage fright. He wrote: "Let's stop calling it 'stage fright' and begin to call 'it' what it is—performance energy. 'Stage fright' sounds scary, overwhelming. Yet it's perfectly natural and it's a good thing to have stage energy."

––––––––––

The lives of these people reveal two important truths: one, anybody can suffer from glossophobia; and two, the power to overcome the fear of public speaking lies in the hands of the individual. Also, being a good public speaker doesn't just stop at overcoming your fear. Whether you are glossophobic or not, you need to learn and know what makes excellent public speaking well, excellent. You need to know the skills, the secrets, the stylistic nuances that come from being behind the microphone.

CHAPTER THREE

How to Speak Like the World's Top Public Speakers

"There are always three speeches, for every one you actually gave. The one you practiced, the one you gave, and the one you wish you gave."

DALE CARNEGIE

There are skills peculiar to every craft. For you to learn and develop a craft, you must imbibe these skills. You must learn the rules and follow them. You may develop your own unique style later, but let the rules of your craft form the foundation for your uniqueness.

As a public speaker who has spoken to many different audiences and also watched and learned from other speakers, I have my own formula for public speaking, which I will share with you in this chapter. But it is important to note that contemporary styles of public speaking are mostly evolutions of the art that hailed from the classical and renaissance eras. The teachings of Aristotle and Cicero on rhetoric shaped the art of public speaking. And so I will use their ideas here as a starting point before delving into my own thoughts. I will also discuss the public speaking strategies of Abraham Lincoln and Winston Churchill, two of the greatest speakers the world has ever known. My aim is to offer you robust knowledge through the fusion of many strategies and styles from different eras—that will guide you into excellent and effective public speaking, as you develop your own style.

Lessons from Aristotle's *The Art of Rhetoric*

"In making a speech one must study three points: first, the means of producing persuasion; second, the language; third the proper arrangement of the various parts of the speech."

ARISTOTLE

As mentioned in Chapter One, Aristotle wrote a treatise on rhetoric which he titled, *The Art of Rhetoric*. It is a three-part work that touches on what Aristotle believed were the key ingredients for effective public speaking. The Aristotelian principles of rhetoric were centered on the art of persuasion, and as I have already stated, public speaking goes beyond just persuasion. But if we examine the other functions of public speaking like education, inspiration and motivation, we will notice that public speaking tries to persuade people to shape their views—either by eliminating old views and embracing new ones, or by broadening the perspectives of already-formed opinions. So in a way, public speaking is form of persuasion, but the key difference now is that the speaker is persuading the audience not for his own benefit, but for theirs. It is for this reason we need to understand The Art of Rhetoric.

The first part of Aristotle's treatise sets forth the general principles, terminologies and assumptions governing rhetoric. The second part is an exposition on the three methods of persuasion: logos (logical reasoning), ethos (character), and pathos (emotion). The final part deals with the style or delivery (lexis) and arrangement (taxis) of rhetoric.

The best public speakers understand and apply these Aristotelian principles to their speeches. So for you to speak like them, you will need to understand and apply them too.

The Art of Rhetoric (Part I)

Lesson 1: Aristotle defines rhetoric as the ability to see what is possibly persuasive in every case. He goes further to define the rhetorician as someone who is always able to see what is persuasive. For Aristotle, rhetoric does not aim to persuade, per se, but seeks to find the appropriate means of persuasion. Aristotle also notes that no one deliberates—or in this case, speaks—about what is certain.

Point 1: **Have insight**. To speak like the world's top public speakers, you must have *insight*. Just as Aristotle said, you can't *ascertain* the minds of the audience, thus you must be able to predict the central desires or conflicts of your audience and tailor your speech towards those desires or conflicts. As a public speaker, one feedback I love receiving from a member(s) of the audience is: "Ron, you spoke directly to me." I am always happy to hear this because it shows that I was able to peek into the minds of the audience to know what they needed to hear. And this brings me to the second lesson.

Point 2: **Know your audience**. To receive insight into what an audience may want to hear starts from knowing the audience. When I am asked to give a speech, I ask questions. Whom am I speaking to? What is the event? What is the average age of members of the audience? What is the economic status of the audience? I analyze my audience with this information at hand. This information lends many clues as to the level of diversity in the audience, and what type of audience I am addressing.

A speech that would be given to a graduating class will be quite different to that which would be presented at a TED talk. A graduating class is a more homogenous audience than a TED audience. The graduating students share similar desires. They want to be assured that, despite going into a tough world, they will win. They need be inspired to never give up on their dreams even when rocked by challenges. They want to be educated on the likely challenges life throws at them after school. On the flip side, members of the TED audience are more interested in social discourse, such as race, religion, politics, gender equality, group economics, the influence of art on the society, and so on. For such a mixed audience, one way to ascertain what the audience wants to hear is to understand the relevance of such discourse at any given *time*.

Point 3: **Understand timing**. Speeches resonate more in the minds of an audience when they touch upon issues affecting the lives of people at a particular point in time. This is why presidents make speeches during times of war, economic turmoil, national disaster, pandemics, and so on. Speeches made in these periods often leave an indelible imprint in the minds of people.

Most of the historical speeches that are still celebrated today were centered on happenings of that period. In 1986 Ronald Reagan addressed the nation when seven astronauts lost their lives while in-flight in the space shuttle Challenger. In 1906, Theodore Roosevelt delivered a speech titled "The Man with the Muck-rake," where he called on journalists to apply moderation and eschew sensationalism in the Progressive Era—which was a period marked by widespread social activism and political reform. In 1942, India was still under the direct rule of Britain, and Mahatma Gandhi delivered an iconic speech asking Britain to "Quit India." In 1940, with the fall of Paris in the Battle of France, England remained Europe's only hope to defeat German Fascism and Nazism; therefore, Winston Churchill had to address the nation to give them hope in their moment of gloom. In 1963, Martin Luther King Jr.'s "I Have a Dream" was written in an effort to instill hope in the black people of America, who were at the time subjugated and treated as lesser beings.

There are many more examples of speeches that addressed conflicts and social issues of the day. Timing always plays an important part in speeches. In fact, the subject of timing is a key aspect of rhetoric, as described by Aristotle. He wrote, "When truth and justice fail through inefficient advocates, the skilled rhetorician will set this right."

The Art of Rhetoric (Part II)

Lesson 2: Aristotle says that because the rhetorician seeks to discern possible means of persuasion, he must rely on proofs. Proofs are of two types: inartistic and artistic proofs. Inartistic proofs are proofs not created by the speaker. They are pre-existing and the speaker applies them to his speech. Examples of these proofs include laws, contracts, oaths, rumors, maxims, proverbs, and testimony of witnesses. Artistic proofs, on the other hand, are created by the speaker, and there are three types: (1) Ethos (ethical), derived from the moral character of the speaker. (2) Pathos (emotional), the speaker tries to put the listener in a certain frame of mind. (3) Logos (logical), a real or apparent truth demonstrated in the speech.

Point 4: **Don't sound empty.** An importance of proofs is that they give robustness to your speech. And a robust speech filled with proofs does two things: (1) it makes your speech more authentic, (2) it shows your audience that you respect their intelligence enough to provide them with relevant proofs for your argument, and you are not just trying to sway them with flowery words.

The *Standard Encyclopaedia of Philosophy* notes that Aristotle's rhetoric is centered on proof because previous theorists of rhetoric were focused on methods outside of the subject; they taught rhetoricians to slander, rouse the emotions of the audience, or distract the audience from the subject.

Members of your audience are not dumb, so don't treat them that way. A conversational speech, for example, may be a question and answer session, and inform you about the audience's wit. But even if the speech isn't conversational, speak to the audience in such a way that they won't feel that their intelligence is being insulted. There are presidents or governors who will address their citizens in a condescending manner to the point where the citizens become angry and outraged at their speeches. People know when a speech is empty, and people know when you are just trying to divert their attention from the current subject. And no one appreciates deflection away from truth. So just offer proofs.

Your proofs can be inartistic. In 2009, Arnold Schwarzenegger delivered a speech titled, "Six Rules of Success," a commencement address at the University of Southern California where Arnold was gifted an honorary degree. In this speech, he used an inartistic proof as his final note of motivation to the graduating students. He said: "This university was conceived in 1880, back when Los Angeles was just a small frontier town. One hundred and twenty-five classes of Trojans have gone before you. They sat here, exactly where you sit today, in good times and in bad, in times of war and in times of peace, in times of great promise and in times of great uncertainty. . . So as you graduate today, never lose that optimism and that fighting spirit. Never lose the spirit of Troy."

The history of the University of California was not invented by Arnold; he only used a preexisting fact to consolidate his points and show why the graduating students must never lose their fighting spirit. Arnold knew that to reorient their minds he would have to go beyond just telling the students to never give up. That would have been too cliché. But by presenting the facts of their school's history, he was able to show them why they should always hold onto the fighting spirit their school was known for. This is how persuasion works.

Another example where inartistic proof was used

was in Barack Obama's address to the nation on September 10, 2013, in which he talked about the civil war in Syria. In the early parts of the speech, Obama speaks about the repressive nature of Syrian's President at the time, Bashar al-Assad who killed over a thousand of his fellow Syrians with poison gas. Obama underscored the terrible nature of chemical weapons—citing how American GIs were killed by a deadly gas in World War I and how "the Nazis used gas to inflict the horror of the Holocaust." These inartistic proofs can be classed as testimonies of witnesses because the world saw and documented these atrocities.

Obama also used another inartistic proof by citing an international law. He said, "Because these weapons can kill on a mass scale with no distinction between soldier and infant, the civilized world has spent a century working to ban them. And in 1997, the United States Senate overwhelmingly approved an international agreement prohibiting the use of chemical weapons, now joined by 189 governments that represent 98 percent of humanity."

Despite the good use of inartistic proofs in his speech, what made Obama's address memorable was his use of artistic proofs.

As a speaker, it is important that you *also offer artistic proofs*. These are proofs created by you. Since these proofs can be presented through ethics, emotions, or logic, they often resonate more than inartistic proofs. In Obama's address that night in September, he used the three forms of artistic proofs to drive home his message—the need for US to attack Syria.

First, there was logos. He outlined the logical reasons as to why the attack was necessary. For instance, he said: "If we fail to act, the Assad regime will see no reason to stop using chemical weapons. As the ban against these weapons erodes, other tyrants will have no reason to think twice about acquiring poison gas, and using them. Over time, our troops will again face the prospect of chemical warfare on the battlefield. And it could be easier for terrorist organizations to obtain these weapons and use them to attack civilians."

Any individual will readily see Obama's point. As a public speaker, your speech must be founded on logical reasoning. Connect the dots of your argument. State why the listener should follow your line of thought. With the world troubled by the Covid-19 pandemic, the WHO and governments aren't just telling the world to stay at home; they are giving the logic behind such an order. "Stay at home to reduce transmission and flatten the curve." It seems logical enough for the people to want to reduce transmission of such a disease. That's logical. And people are heeding the order because they understand the logic behind it and wish to do the "right thing."

In his speech, Obama analyzed the current situation (recall what we talked about with timing) and presented the possible implications if Assad wasn't called to order. In the latter parts of this speech, he explained that the ramifications were far-reaching and could spill into other parts of the world. However, to strengthen his position, Obama used his next means of persuasion: ethos.

He told the people of the United States that his position as the President of the United States offered him the power to make decisions that were best for the United States and the world at large. However, this doesn't translate to him sidelining Congress.

Here were his exact words: "That's my judgment as Commander-in-Chief. But I'm also the President of the world's oldest constitutional democracy. So even though I possess the authority to order military strikes, I believed it was right, in the absence of a direct or imminent threat to our security, to take this debate to Congress. I believe our democracy is stronger when the President acts with the support of Congress."

Obama's position as POTUS gave credibility to his speech. He let the nation know that he was in the position to make crucial decisions for the greater good of humankind. Towards the end of his address, Obama eluded to the weight of his presidency, stating that "the burdens of leadership are often heavy, but the world is a better place because we have borne them."

Imagine if it were Mark Zuckerberg addressing the nation on the need to attack another country: do you think the people would agree with his decision? Of course not. Many would question Zuckerberg's authority, because he is not a political figure, therefore the rationality behind his decision would be questioned. Even if what he was saying was rational, many would still doubt if he had weighed the possible outcomes of such a decision, a decision we trust more to those holding seat with presidential powers. People would readily listen to Zuckerberg if, however, he gave a speech about say, technology, and the role of AI in today's world. Because, simply put, Zuckerberg's authority lies in technology, not politics.

During the Covid-19 pandemic, the world has looked to the World Health Organization for solutions. As a matter of fact, Covid-19 was not called a pandemic until the WHO declared it to be one. No president has yet to declare it a pandemic either, despite the ravaging effects the virus is having on the state of the world, as it currently spreads throughout China, Europe and North America. This is the power in and of authority.

It is far easier to persuade your audience when you present yourself as an authority on the subject. In the previous chapter, I talked about "The Iron Lady of Pakistan," Muniba Mazari Baloch. One is motivated and inspired by Muniba's speech she delivers on withstanding adversity, because it is evident that she has experienced the adversity herself, and has come out all the stronger for it. Her story, albeit a sad one, has given her the authority to speak on such issues.

A friend of mine, a medical doctor and a content

writer, was invited to a webinar to speak on content writing and marketing. Beside his name on the flier were the words, "Doctor & Content Writer." He asked the organizers to take out "Doctor" and leave only "Content Writer." True, he is doctor, but he wasn't there to speak on medicine at the webinar, he was there to speak on the subject of content writing. He knew that the audience would more readily accept his teachings more if he presented himself as a content writer, rather than as a doctor cum content writer. Presenting himself *only* as a content writer sells the notion to the audience that he has committed all his time and resources to this specific career path. This focus then strengthens his authority on the subject, unlike the title of 'doctor and content writer.' . People know how demanding medical practice is, so the audience would think that the demand that comes with being a doctor would dilute or outweigh his commitment to content writing, even though we know this is probably not the case.

Your authority is a vital tool in your public speaking toolbox. Do not fail to use it when you can. If there is no opportunity to use it, then you should now consider appealing to the emotions of your audience. This is where pathos comes in.

Barack Obama talked about the questions and concerns he had received regarding the issues with Syria. Many of these concerns were valid: some feared that the attack would lead to a war; others asked if the attack was worth it, while yet others were of the opinion that the US shouldn't interfere in the business of other countries. To address these concerns, Obama appealed to the emotions of Americans by creating vivid images of the devastations that lay ahead if Assad was allowed to thrive.

Obama said: "And so, to my friends on the right; I ask you to reconcile your commitment to America's military might with a failure to act when a cause is so plainly just. To my friends on the left; I ask you to reconcile your belief in freedom and dignity for all people with those images of children writhing in pain, and going still on a cold hospital floor. For, sometimes resolutions and statements of condemnation are simply not enough."

These words drew the mind of the audience back to the descriptions of massacre Obama had painted at the beginning of the address. He spoke of men, women, children lying in rows killed by poison gas; of people foaming at the mouth, gasping for breath; of a father clutching his dead children, imploring them to get up and walk.

Obama employed the horror of these images to create sadness, pity, and then anger in the hearts of listeners. People would naturally react with horror, wondering, "How could someone be so wicked? These innocent people don't deserve this. Assad needs to be taken out!" Obama's use of logic here was laced with persuasive pathos. He told the country that if Assad wasn't stopped, other tyrants would take it as a cue to perpetrate vile acts that would spill into other countries, including the US. And, he knew that by delivering such information he was capable of creating fear. And since fear is the primal emotion to spur us towards protection and self preservation, Americans would have a hard time disagreeing with Obama's stance on the matter, and would be more likely to act in support of their President, trusting that he knew what was best for their national security.

As a public speaker, appealing to the emotions

of your audience is an essential skill.. Humans are emotional species. We are distinct from other animals because we are rational. And rationality means having the emotions *and* the intelligence to control these emotions. We feel anger, fear, sadness, happiness, disgust, surprise, shock, empathy, sympathy, shame, guilt, grief, horror, pity, pride, rage, remorse, and so many other emotions that heighten our understanding of the world.

People have obeyed the Covid-19 stay-at-home orders because their emotions have been appealed to throughout the entire process. Firstly, people were *shocked* about the rapid infection and death rates. Then they *feared* contracting the virus, being sick, and infecting their loved ones. Then they *feared* losing a loved one to the pandemic. They understood the burden of *guilt* they would have to carry if a friend or family member contracted the disease because they refused to obey the orders. And they didn't want to *grieve* over a loved one, or carry the burden of guilt for infecting another person. The weight of social responsibility, therefore, has been placed on the person to 'do the right thing,' using pathos to appeal to, and persuade civilians.

So it becomes necessary to employ emotions if you want to cement your message in the minds of your audience. Take them through an emotional journey. If you want to encourage them to go for their goals, take them through a bittersweet tale of a person who faced challenges and overcame life's obstacles to achieve such goals If you want to incite people to take action against an unjust system, make them angry with the status quo. If you want them to change a behavior, create guilt—and maybe fear too—by showing them the dangers of the behavior—then having them imagining the joy and pride they'd feel if they changed.

Appealing to emotions is vital for effective public speaking. After all, Maya Angelou said, "People will forget what you said, people will forget what you did, but people will never forget how you made them feel."

The Art of Rhetoric (Part III)

Lesson 3: Aristotle emphasizes the importance of lexis (style) and taxis (arrangement). On style, he says it is not sufficient to know <u>what</u> to say, you must know <u>how</u> to say it. The speaker should know how to manage his voice—employing tones and rhythms. This is the bedrock of delivery and the element of rhetoric Aristotle considers most important.

Point 5: **Use your voice to convey emotion**. Your voice is your most important asset in public speaking. Use it well. It was Maya Angelou who noted that, "Words mean more than what is set down on paper. It takes the human voice to infuse them with deeper meaning." The ability of your audience to feel the emotions and power of your words lies in how you use your voice. Richard Branson may have likened public speaking to a conversation with a friend, but when it comes to using your voice, you don't speak to your audience as if you are speaking to a friend.

When you are with your friend you can choose to converse in whispers or you can be as loud as you want, depending on your environment. In conversations, you don't pay attention to the tone of your voice; you just talk and focus only on the message. However, in public speaking, you have to consider how the tone of your voice changes. If you pass the right message with a wrong tone, your audience may not pay attention.

With the right voice, you can get into the heads of your audience and implant your message in their minds. Adolf Hitler was one of the vilest men that ever lived, yet we cannot ignore the fact that he knew how to employ public speaking to get Germans to believe in his evil causes. In *Mein Kampf,* Hitler wrote "I know that men are won over less by the written than by the spoken word, that every great movement on this earth owes its growth to great orators and not to great writers." And he is not wrong. Experts who have analyzed Hitler's speeches reveals that his voice was a key ingredient in the 5,000 plus speeches the Führer used to persuade and bewitch his audiences.

Amanda Macias in a *Business Insider* article writes that, in the book, *Explaining Hitler*, Ron Rosenbaum quoted George Steiner, a French-American novelist, to have described Hitler's voice as "overwhelmingly powerful" and "spellbinding." Steiner said that Hitler's voice was a hard thing to describe; it was "mesmeric." "The amazing thing is that the body comes through on the radio. I can't put it any other way. You feel you're following the gestures," said Steiner.

You may write the perfect speech, but if you don't use your voice correctly, your speech will just be another average, easily-forgotten presentation. Read these words aloud:

> *"I have a dream that one day this nation will rise up and live out the true meaning of its creed. . . I have a dream that my four little children will one day live in a nation where they will not be judged by the color of their skin but by the content of their character. I have a dream today."*

If you have listened to Martin Luther King Jr.'s speech, it is almost impossible for you to read these words aloud in your voice. You'd want to sound like him—high-pitched and energetic. We remember this speech—and particularly this quote—not just for the power in the words, but in the tone in which they were conveyed. Imagine if Martin Luther King Jr. had said those words in a dull manner, lacking energy? I doubt if we would still remember this speech today. The buoyant tone of King's words conveyed the inspiration, motivation and hope he aimed to deliver through his speech.

Use the appropriate pace for your speech. Don't be too fast, don't be too slow. Let your audience *appreciate* each word, each sentence. In their course, "Principles of Public Speaking," Lumen Learning notes that speaking too quickly will: (1) Give the audience the impression that you have nothing important to say. (I concur with this: if you have something important to say you won't rush through it. You'll allow your audience the chance to *listen* to you.) (2) Make it difficult for the audience to comprehend what you are saying. (3) Give the audience the impression that you never wanted to speak in the first place (and that maybe you were cajoled into giving the speech, or you have a more important event to catch up with.)

On the flip side, Lumen Learning also states that speaking too slowly will: (1) Give the audience the impression that you are too tired to speak. (2) Make the audience lose interest in the speech as they will forget the first part of your sentence by the time you get to the last. (3) Make the audience feel you are only there to waste their time.

So maintain a balance. For *effect* and *emphasis*, slow down parts of your speech. But this shouldn't be done frequently.

> *Lesson 4: Aristotle writes that one of the excellences of style is clearness or perspicuity. Speech, if it does not make the meaning clear, will not perform its proper function.*

Point 6: **Let your speech be clear**. As a writer and public speaker, I don't fancy the use of many of big words in speech and writing. Big words have the tendency of making a speech or writing sound flowery and too wordy. Now, I am not saying the use of big words are inappropriate; what I'm saying is that using them *too* much in your work might make your work lose form and meaning. I have listened to speakers and read writers who feel that sounding grandiloquent makes their audience perceive them as being smarter. In truth, the audience may perceive them that way, but the fact is that the aim of communication will be lost in the process.

A speech bereft of clarity is almost, if not, valueless to the listener. Remember the aim of speaking is to persuade—to inspire, motivate, encourage, educate, incite. If none of these is achieved because your audience found your speech too difficult to comprehend, then of what use was speaking in the first place?

If you ever want to get carried away by florid speaking (or writing; because most times, we write our speeches before presenting them), remember these quotes culled by Richard Nordquist in his *ThoughtCo* article, "What Is Clarity in Composition?"

> *"When asked what qualities they value most in writing, people who read a great deal professionally put clarity at the top of their list. If they have to invest too much effort in figuring out the writer's meaning, they will give up in dismay or annoyance."*
>
> **MAXINE C. HAIRSTON,**
>
> *SUCCESSFUL WRITING*. **NORTON, 1992.**

"It is bad manners to give [readers] needless trouble. Therefore clarity [is to be achieved mainly] by taking trouble and by writing to serve people rather than to impress them."

F. L. LUCAS, *STYLE.* **CASSELL, 1955.**

"For any kind of public speaking, as for any kind of literary communication, clarity is the highest beauty."

HUGHES OLIPHANT OLD,

THE READING AND PREACHING OF THE SCRIPTURES.

WM. B. EERDMANS, 2004.

Lesson 5: For Aristotle, the language should have a "foreign" air, something removed from the commonplace; for men admire what is remote, and that which excites admiration is pleasant.

Point 7: **Let your speech have a literary flavor.** Some speakers and writers have taken this to mean having big vocabularies that are difficult to grasp on the spot. The "foreignness" of speech is not the same as the floridness of speech. A speech can be foreign, yet clear and simple.

This is what you should aim for as a public speaker. Check the greatest speeches of all time, and you will discover that they are easy to understand and still have a literariness to them.

The literary flavor of your speech is what distinguishes you from your audience. Someone who is not a public speaker would care less about the sound or beauty of his sentences. He just speaks plainly. But you do not have this "luxury" as a speaker; you must make a conscious effort to adorn your speeches with literary devices like metaphors and similes. For instance, in JFK's inaugural address Kennedy said: "The energy, the faith, the devotion which we bring to this endeavor will light our country and all who serve it. And the glow from that fire can truly light the world." JFK used a metaphor to equate the energy, faith and devotion of Americans to a fire which would light the country so bright that its glow would light the world. This metaphor has a nice ring to it and creates a much more vivid image than if Kennedy had simply said, "Our collective efforts to uphold freedom will have a positive impact in our country and also the rest of the world."

Also, in the same speech he used another literary

device namely antithesis, when he said: "Let us never negotiate out of fear, but let us never fear to negotiate." Sharp and witty. Weaving the first statement into the second lends a musical quality to his statement and achieves three things: he makes a profound statement in few words, retains the full meaning of his message, and he makes his message resonate. Imagine if he had only said, "We will never negotiate out of fear. However, we will also not shy away from negotiation."

So pepper your speeches with literary devices—from metaphor to simile, assonance to alliteration, antithesis to rhetorical questions. However, do not overuse them. They are the spices, not the main dish.

Also, the literariness of your speeches includes rhythm. Let your speech be rhythmical but not too rhythmical that it sounds like a poem or a spoken word presentation. Just have the right rhythm and cadence to help with the flow of the speech. Aristotle puts it this way: "Prose should not be metrical, but must have rhythm. Meter distracts the listener, while the absence of rhythm creates unpleasantness and obscurity." One sure way of getting the right flow for your speech is by arranging your ideas.

Lesson 6: On arrangement, Aristotle writes that there are two necessary parts of a speech: (1) <u>statement</u> of the case, (2) <u>proof</u>. To these, one may also add <u>exordium</u>—the beginning of a speech, similar to a prologue; and <u>epilogue</u>—which he says is not always necessary.

Point 8: **Have a pattern of flow**. Your ideas should not be disjointed lest you lose the attention of your audience. I consider public speaking as the telling of a story, taking an audience on a journey. Thus, it is important for there to be an orderly flow of information. You are trying to persuade the people; this is why Aristotle talked about first *stating* the case, only then providing *proof*.

For example, this is the skeletal framework of Obama's national address we analyzed earlier:

Statement of the case: The crisis in Syria and the vile actions of Assad.

Proofs: The casualties. The need for America to act. The implications if America does not act.

Another example: the framework for Arnold Schwarzenegger's "6 Rules of Success" has all four elements outlined by Aristotle:

Exordium: Note: Although he started his address with some preambles like appreciating the school for conferring him the honorary degree, I consider the speech to have begun after the preambles.

Schwarzenegger began his speech by telling the students he was addressing them as a new member of the Trojan family. Then he continued to say that his daughter just enrolled into the school, and while his daughter's academic life was just beginning, theirs was ending. He went on to say that while some people thought it scary to leave the comfort of university days, he believed that the graduating students were at an advantage being American, in a country filled with opportunity, and that they had no need to worry.

Statement of the case: Arnold stated that although they were surrounded by opportunities, it was important to realize there would be setbacks, failures or disappointments. So he was gifting them by imparting some of his ideas on how to be successful.

Proofs: He shared his personal stories of his uneasy road to success, first as a bodybuilder, then actor, then governor.

Epilogue: He reminded them that they were USC

Trojans, so they shouldn't lose their fighting spirit. They should be proud, strong and ready to soar.

Presenting your speech with a clear structure makes it easier to understand and remember. For example, I wrote the skeletal framework of Obama and Schwarzenegger's speeches without going back to listen to them. This is because I knew how they started their speech, how they presented their ideas, and how they ended it. If these speeches were disjointed, they would have lacked clarity, and it would have been difficult to remember them.

Salespersons and marketers understand this well and have developed series of formulas to ensure that their marketing techniques follows a logical pattern to persuade prospective buyers. The most popular of these formulas is AIDA which stands for *Attention, Interest, Desire, and Action.* This formula can be placed side by side with Aristotle's formula of *Exordium, Statement, Proof, and Epilogue.*

The different parts of a speech are a family united by a central idea. Your exordium, statement of the case, proofs, and epilogue must focus on your common idea(s). You can use examples or stories to support your speech but you must ensure that these examples are related to the subject. For example, when Obama referred to the First and Second World Wars in his speech, he touched only on the effects of the abuse of chemical weapons. He knew every weapon had the potential to be abused, but since Assad used sarin gas, a chemical weapon, to kill hundreds of innocents, Obama stuck only to that aspect of weaponry—from the beginning to the end of his speech.

The Five Canons of Rhetoric by Cicero

"When you wish to instruct, be brief; that men's minds take in quickly what you say, learn its lesson, and retain it faithfully. Every word that is unnecessary only pours over the side of a brimming mind."

CICERO

The Ciceronian five canons of rhetoric are another set of approaches that have been employed by public speakers, past and present. These canons were outlined by Cicero in his handbook for orators titled, *De Inventione*. Although Cicero considered *De Inventione* obsolete in comparison to his later works, the canons are still an important contribution to the art of rhetoric and public speaking.

It is important to note that it was Quintilian who organized Cicero's treatise on oratory into what is today as the five canons of rhetoric. The five canons are *inventio* (invention), *dispositio* (arrangement), *elocutio* (style or expression), *memoria* (memory), and *pronuntiatio* (delivery). You will notice that some of these canons overlap with elements of Aristotle's treatise. So while I am going to explain these canons individually, I will only focus on the ways Cicero differs to Aristotle here.

> *Canon 1: Invention. Cicero says this is the central, most important canon. It is the systematic search for arguments. It is the process of coming up with materials for your speech, and it echoes Aristotle's belief that rhetoric should be more focused on finding the means of persuasion more than the act of persuasion itself.*

Point 9: **Brainstorm**. This is the most important part of public speaking. While scholars have shown the similarities between Cicero's "invention" and Aristotle's "means of persuasion," I am of the opinion that the two are quite different. Aristotle's methods of persuasion employ different techniques the speaker can use to sell his message to his audience. But in invention, the speaker creates something out of nothing, or something out of something. Simply put, the speaker produces the topic or subject matter.

Sometimes, speakers face the challenge of not knowing what to say. In the writing world this is called writer's block. However, an effective way of overcoming this challenge is to focus on timing. What is the current situation of your environment? Certain periods of the year are marked by certain events. For instance, in 2017, the #MeToo movement gained traction after sexual abuse allegations were leveled at Harvey Weinstein. In 2018, issues surrounding climate change became a matter of global discourse. In 2019, there were more sexual abuse allegations, more climate change issues, and more cases of police brutality than ever before in recorded history. Cases of police brutality have even spilled over into 2020 alongside the worldwide Covid-19 pandemic.

Now, as a public speaker, depending on your audience and event, you could choose to tailor your speech to the happenings of a particular period and relate them to the real world in real time. Trending issues come with diverse narratives; thus, as a speaker, you have a duty to find the common ground among these narratives and show your audience the true path.

Another way to invent a topic is by sharing a personal story. We have seen earlier how Muniba Mazari Baloch rendered a powerful speech by telling her own story. Also, Rami Elhanan—an Israeli, and Bassam Aramin—a Palestinian, are two fathers who travel the world sharing the sad stories of how they lost their daughters in the Israeli-Palestinian conflict. Smadar, the daughter of Rami was killed in 1997 by a Palestinian suicide bomber; while Abir, the daughter of Bassam was killed in 2007 by a rubber bullet shot by an Israeli soldier. The girls were thirteen and ten years old respectively when they died. The two fathers have become renowned public speakers, sharing the same stories in an effort to drive home the global need for peace, unity and love in these unstable times.

When inventing your speech, ensure you do not err on the side of controversy or sensationalism. I consider this a huge turn off when it comes to public speaking. Aim to present your points just as they are. Don't exaggerate it. Keep it plausible. On plausibility, Cicero wrote: "The narrative will be plausible if it seems to embody characteristics which are accustomed to appear in real life, if the proper qualities of the character are maintained, if reasons for their actions are plain, if there seems to have been ability to do the deed, if it can be shown that the time was opportune, the space sufficient and the place suitable for the events about to be narrated."

Invention deals with brainstorming. The truth is all stories have been told, so you have to look for a new way to tell your story.

Canon 2: Arrangement. This is how a speech is arranged. While Aristotle divided a speech into two major parts, Cicero suggested that a speech have six parts:

exordium (the introduction),
narratio (statement of the problem), partitio/divisio (outline of major points), confirmatio (the proof of the case), confutatio/reprehensio (refutation of opposing arguments), and
peroratio (conclusion).

These parts of speech have been already seen in discussing the Aristotelian art of rhetoric. However, for the sake of brevity and lack of repetition I will focus here on only one of part, confutatio or reprehensio.

Point 10: **Address opposing views**. In public speaking, it is not enough to tell your audience why they should act a certain way, you should also be able to tell them why they should understand and accept your views and not those of another. (By "another" I mean either themselves or someone else.) We saw this in Obama's address to the nation on Syria and Assad's dictatorship. Barack Obama didn't just outline why it was imperative that Assad be stopped; he also took time to talk about the divergent views he had received and his answers addressing these views.

Refuting opposing arguments adds robustness to your speech and informs your audience that your ideas on the subject are comprehensive. Let's say you are to give a speech on depression; a speech which is geared to inspire people and intended to deter them from taking their life. Your first thought will likely be to talk about how there is more to life than sadness; how there is hope at the end of the day, how they are beautiful, blessed and loved, how death is not the answer. Yes, all of these are cool. But you haven't countered or entertained any of the opposing views depressed or potentially suicidal victims really have. People contemplating suicide believe that living is weakness, while dying is bravery. Some also believe they are hardwired towards depression. Yet others think that no form of therapy is the best approach when dealing with thoughts of suicide. These are all strong, opposing views—and they have the power to dilute the effects of your wonderful speech. So you have to be prepared to counter them, if your argument is to carry any weight.

Countering opposing views offers intelligent thought to your speech. There are subjects that have become too commonplace and boring because the topic has been discussed ad nauseum and exhausted by the same stuff being said over and over again. However, if you want to know the different views on a subject and feel confident enough to incorporate these views into your speech, there is a greater likelihood that your speech will be one your audience has never heard before.

> *Canon 3: Style/Expression. This is the fitting of the proper language to the invented matter. This deals with vocabulary choices, sentence structure and expressions used in the speech. There are three levels of style: plain, middle, and high. According to Quintilian, the plain style is most suitable for instruction, middle for moving oration, and high for charming discourse. To achieve a good style, a speech must be <u>correct</u>, <u>clear</u>, <u>appropriate</u> and <u>ornamented</u>.*

We have looked at the use of language earlier, focusing on the use of a variety of literary devices to give your speech a "foreign" air. However, Cicero's additions on style, expressions and language also come in handy for the public speaker.

Point 11: **Use balanced expressions or style.** According to Richard Nordquist, a plain style is a speech that is simple, direct and straightforward. Cicero likened the plain style to women who look more beautiful when unadorned. For Cicero, the style "gives pleasure when unembellished." The language is plain and clear, and propriety is the chief aim.

Nordquist also defines high or grand style in speech as one characterized by "a heightened emotional tone, imposing diction, and highly ornate figures of speech." Cicero described it as magnificent, stately, opulent and ornate.

Middle style falls between the plain and high style, and this is the style I advise speakers to go for. Speech is not the same as writing. In a book, the reader has enough time to digest what is being read; sadly this is not the case with a speech. If you have thirty minutes to make a speech, the audience must understand and digest your every word within those minutes, and in real time.

Therefore, using a high or grand style may make your speech too lofty or difficult to grasp. Your speech will be filled with flowery words that have no substance and communicate no message beyond your ability to show off a grand vocabulary. On the other hand, a plain style may make your speech *too* elementary and without enough "foreign" quality. So the middle is best: communicate as clearly as possible, and adorn your speech in the right places.

> *Canon 4: Memory. This involves recalling the arguments of a discourse. Simply put, it is recalling or memorizing your speech. This goes beyond rote learning, as it also involves improvisation. Memory, as a canon, has three elements: memorizing your speech as a speaker, making your speech memorable, and keeping a treasury of rhetorical fodder.*

Point 12: **Own your speech**. Imagine you are in the audience listening to a speaker delivering a speech and all through the speech he never takes his eyes off his note. What perception would you have of that speaker? You would easily arrive at one of the following conclusions: either he lacks confidence, he never wrote the speech, or he is reading a speech on behalf of another. Whatever the case, it will greatly affect the overall quality of the speech.

As a public speaker, you must memorize your speech. This shows the audience that you *own* the speech. Memorizing your speech doesn't mean you won't also access your notes while on stage, but it results in being less dependent on notes, taking only *occasional* glances at your paper, which not only increases your credibility—but builds your ethos as a speaker.

Furthermore, memorizing your speech as a speaker shouldn't be cause for you to robotically regurgitate your speech, spitting it out word for word exactly as you've memorized it. Make room for improvisation. I have been to events, especially academic lectures, where a speaker needed to project his subject onto a screen. I am always impressed with the speaker who is able to speak and explain his topic without using the exact words on the screen. This demonstrates clear ownership of the subject matter. It also informs the audience that the speaker takes his invention process seriously. A speech becomes part of you when you invent it yourself. As you study and research your topic, you will come across concepts that may not be part of the original idea of your speech, but these additional points can help validate your proofs.

In addition, memory also involves your audience. In this book I have stressed the importance of making your speech resonate with your audience. Make your speech memorable. The greatest speeches of all time are great because they stayed in the minds of the listeners. Let your words stick. This will cement your authority as an excellent public speaker.

Finally, top public speakers understand that they will, from time to time, be called upon to speak. So, one speech effectively creates material for the next. I recall the Jamaican novelist, Nicole Dennis-Benn saying in an interview that the world exists in her head, so her readers are bound to see a character from a previous novel reappear in a new one. You can adopt this approach with your speeches. Make your speeches raw material for future speeches. Use or invent quotes, facts, or stories that can come in handy in other speeches.

Fusing the three elements of memory together,

we could say that memory applies to the speaker, the audience, and the speech itself.

Canon 5: Delivery. This involves voice and gestures during speaking. It includes the proper modulation of voice, phrasing, pace, emphasis of speech, stance, gestures, posture, and facial expressions.

Point 13: **Be pleasant and confident.** Let your posture show you are confident. Don't droop. Stand tall with poise, and with grace. Quintilian sums up the subject of posture in his *Institutio Oratoria*; in it, he wrote: "The head, being the chief member of the body, has a corresponding importance in delivery, serving not merely to produce graceful effect, but to illustrate our meaning as well. To secure grace, it is essential that the head should be carried naturally and erect. For a droop suggests humility, while if it be thrown back it seems to express arrogance, if inclined to one side it gives an impression of languor, while if it is held too stiffly and rigidly it appears to indicate a rude and savage temper."

In addition to your posture, your facial expression should be pleasant. Don't smile too much, lest you are not taken seriously. Also don't frown or scowl lest you scare your audience. Your facial expression should reveal the emotions behind each part of your speech. You are the first beneficiary of your speech, so convey the emotions you want your audience to feel—not only through your words and tone, but also through facial expressions. When a part of your speech is humorous, smile or laugh. If it is saddening, frown. If it is matter-of-fact, let the seriousness of the statement be written on your face.

The emotions you show should be *genuine*. There are people who have delivered speeches so emotional that they burst into tears on stage. Genuine emotions can only be revealed when your speech is a part of you, and you are a part of your speech.

I have developed these 11 points of public speaking from two of the greatest scholars of rhetoric and public speaking. However, I also have my personal strategies for effective public speaking based on my experience and study. These strategies were first published as a blog post; but more has to be said, and this book now affords me the opportunity to say more, to write more, and to share more

How to Speak Like the World's Top Public Speakers in 11 Suggestions

Tip 1: Get out of your head and get in your heart. Leave your ego at the door.

One interesting quality about writers is the way they cherish their works. I have heard writers, especially novelists, refer to their works as their babies; they often have an emotional attachment to them. This is because writers write from their hearts. They pour all of themselves into their writing. This is what you should do with your speeches.

When writing your speech, write from your heart. And when delivering the speech, deliver it with all of your heart. Let your words inspire you, too. You are your first audience.

World-class speakers talk on subjects they are passionate about, skilled in, have achieved remarkable results in, and/or carried out extensive research on. They have a depth of understanding or experience in the subject.

During your invention stage, go for topics you are passionate about. Even in cases where you are given a theme to speak on, find a way to weave in what you are passionate about into your speech. When you listen to world-class speakers, you discover that their speeches have recurring themes. Barack Obama's speeches are centered on the importance of Americans understanding one another and working together, eschewing division, improving society, and protecting democracy. Brian Tracy focuses on leadership, selling, self-esteem, goals, strategy, creativity, and success. Les Brown talks about achieving goals, overcoming odds, wealth, and destiny, and so on.

However, in a case where you are required to speak on a subject you are not familiar with, carry out extensive research on the subject till it becomes a part of you. Never deny yourself the opportunity of speaking with your heart. Study the unfamiliar topic. Digest it. Love it. Seek opinions about it. Know the right emotions to be conveyed along with the message you are trying to pass on.

Also, don't let your ego get in the way of developing a connection with your speech. Your ego can interfere in two ways: a bloated ego feels too big, too important to show emotions; while a deflated ego feels too timid, too ashamed to show emotions.

A speech not written and delivered from the heart sounds mechanical and boring. This is not a desirable trait; nor is it a trait of world-class speakers. No world-class speaker ever sounds boring. You can feel the passion and emotion pouring out of their every word, and they have the ability to make even the dullest topic sound interesting.

Just as you would cradle your baby and present your child to the world, you need to present your speech in a such a way that everyone knows it has birthed from your heart.

Tip 2: Remind yourself that speaking is not all about you, it's about creating value for your audience.

I have likened a speech to a child. It is true that parents love their children and are protective of them, however, they know that they have a duty to train their children to become responsible members of the society. It is their job to train their children to add value to the society. One reason parents try not to raise spoilt brats is so that the child won't become a societal nuisance. If the child is spoilt, the parents may be able to handle the situation—but would society be able to do the same?

Why have I drawn this analogy? Your speech is not only about you: it is also about your audience. In fact, it is more about your audience than it is about you. So while you develop a connection to your speeches, they must add value to your audience. Don't leave a sentence that you know won't be comprehensible to your audience just because you like how the sentence rings. Don't use a high style when you clearly know your audience won't appreciate a flamboyant speech. Don't talk about an idea or issue that will make your audience uncomfortable just because it is part of your belief. Don't stir up unnecessary controversies. Add value.

Furthermore, don't just provide information, offer insights. Information is common and does not carry as much value as insights. When John F. Kennedy in his inaugural address said, "Ask not what your country can do for you — ask what you can do for your country," he didn't just give us information; he offered a great insight. Citizens often get carried away with their complaints of what the country doesn't and hasn't done for them. Seldom do citizens stop and think about ways they could make their country better. But JFK's speech was capable of making citizens think about something the likes they had probably never thought of, which at that time, was groundbreaking

Without insights, you cannot spur people into action. Insights are so powerful that even a villain can use it to stir negative action. Adolf Hitler's insights stirred his people so much that it incited them against the Jews. In his opinion piece in the *New York Times*, Timothy Snyder notes that Hitler was a propagandist, a pioneer of "fake news." He used his speeches to show Germans a "truth" that never existed.. For Hitler, Snyder writes, "Everything that might seem to be a higher goal ("religion, socialism, democracy") was for Jews a way to make to make money. Jews were not to be treated as fellow people, but to be understood as an objective problem, like a disease ("racial tuberculosis") that needed to be resolved. . . *All ideas of universal goodness were simply mental traps set by Jews to catch weak German brains. The only way to restore German faith and virtue was through the physical elimination and eradication of the Jews.*"

I emphasize these last two sentences because it was these sentences that formed the core of Hitler's insights. Being insightful means offering new truths, new perspectives, and persuading others to accept these truths. Hitler told the Germans they were being mentally exploited by the Jews; and that the *only* way to remedy the situation was to exterminate them. This is of course untrue. But Hitler was able to persuade and convince the Germans to accept his propaganda. Citing Benjamin Carter, Snyder writes that, "the key to understanding why many Germans supported [him] lies in the Nazi's total rejection of a rational, factual world." They rejected one world and accepted another because the former world gave them nothing new (or so they thought), while the new world Hitler presented them with promised mental liberation as long as they did what was needful.

This is the strength of insightful speeches. If insights can be used to twist the minds of one race against another and exterminate millions of people, it can also be used to propagate positive narratives.

In addition to giving insights, another way you can use your speech to add value is by seeking out a problem and attempting to solve it. This is what world-class speakers do. I have heard many complain about motivational speakers—how their speeches are filled with clichés, how they give a temporary feel-good effect. And I have discovered that the reason behind why people make these complaints is because the clichéd motivational speaking never solves any problem.

How do you tell people that they can make it, they can take charge of their destinies, they can rise above their challenges—without telling them how they can do these things? Do not make blanket statements. A speech shouldn't be a one-size-fits-all approach that is used and reused across events. A better approach would be to know the possible reasons why people aren't successful, why they are incapable of rising above challenges, and then proffering solutions to overcoming them.

Using Obama's speech again as an example: Imagine if he had just stated the problems in Syria without offering any solution. Imagine if he had talked about disciplining Assad without allaying the fears of Americans with regards to the possible implications of such actions?

Don't just aim to inspire or motivate; aim to transform, aim to to provide solutions.

Bonus tip: Let your speech be insightful. Look for the hidden information that everyone seems to miss and come up with a topic that is either unconventional, has a unique twist, or challenges the status quo. Also, when you speak, talk about a relevant issue or problem that people are facing and struggling to solve.

Tip 3: Have a powerful and impactful opening

The chorus of Anna Kendrick's cover of "Cups" plays in the background. "You're gonna miss me when I'm gone." Obama steps to the podium as the audience applause fades, saying, "You can't say it, but you know it's true." The audience laughs.

This was the opening of Barack Obama's speech at the White House Correspondents' Dinner in 2016. He fused his impending exit from the oval office with Anna

Kendrick's song to pass a strong, opening message to his audience, albeit with sentimental humor.

Earlier, I emphasized the importance of timing, and here I will do so again. Public speakers are not afforded the luxury of time that a writer has. There are books that drag at the beginning and become more interesting as you get halfway through. The writer has an unlimited amount of time to woo and win readers with his words. But as a public speaker, you have only a *limited* time to create a *memorable* impression in the minds of your audience. And having a powerful opening is a good way to start.

Aristotle, Cicero, and Quintilian placed much emphasis on on exordium, the beginning of your speech. However, one thing they didn't note was the creativity that is needed in opening a speech. Find the most creative way to get your audience hooked. Get their attention with your opening and they will be glued to their seats to hear the rest of what you will say. Never start your speech with bland expressions like, "Thank you," "Good morning," or "I'm so happy to be here."

The opening of your speech is not limited to words

alone; your appearance, a prop, a song, or a video can be used to create a memorable opening. Here are some methods you can use to create a powerful opening.

- **Words**: This could be through:

Humor, as we saw in Obama's speech at the correspondents' dinner.

Imagination, like in Ric Elias' TED talk titled, "3 Things I Learned While My Plane Crashed." Elias' speech began like this: "Imagine a big explosion as you climb to 3,000 ft. Imagine a plane full of smoke. Imagine an engine going clack, clack, clack. It sounds scary. Well I had a unique seat that day. I was sitting in 1D."
Elias created an image in the minds of his audience. This image was scary. In that moment, I think most people in the audience had to have been thinking about what they would have done, had they found themselves in such a situation. And this imagination, this fear, this questioning, provided the perfect foundation upon which Elias

built his speech.

Questions, like in Simon Sinek's TED Talk, "How Great Leaders Inspire Action." Sinek began his speech by asking: *"How do you explain when things don't go as we assume? Or better, how do you explain when others are able to achieve things that seem to defy all of the assumptions?"*

Sinek asked his audience a profound question. And as they pondered that thought, he began his speech.

Suspense, like Dan Pink did in his TED Talk, "The Puzzle of Motivation." Pink, rubbed his palms together, as if nervous, and said: "I need to make a confession at the outset here. Little over 20 years ago, I did something that I regret. Something that I'm not particularly proud of. Something that in many ways I wish no one would ever know, but that here I feel kind of obliged to reveal."

Pink created suspense with these words. Rubbing his palms even heightened the suspense. If you were in the audience, wouldn't you be wondering what this confession might be? Did he kill someone? Did he do drugs? Was he arrested for drunk driving?

Even now, reading this, I'm sure you're eager to know what Pink said.

Storytelling, like in Steve Jobs commencement address at Stanford University. Jobs began with: "I never graduated from college. Truth be told, this is the closest I've ever gotten to a college graduation. Today I want to tell you three stories from my life. That's it. No big deal. Just three stories. The first story is about connecting the dots. I dropped out of Reed College after the first 6 months, but then stayed around as a drop-in for another 18 months or so before I really quit. So why did I drop out?" Everybody loves a good story. So when you open with one, the audience will be hooked, eager to know where the story leads.

Provocative statements, like Larry Smith's, "I want to discuss with you this afternoon why you're going to fail to have a great career." This is the way he started his TEDx speech titled, "Why You Will Fail To Have A Great Career."

This opening is a blend of provocation and suspense. As a listener, you would be questing, "Why would he say I'd fail at having a great career?" And for you to know why the statement was made, you would have to listen on.

- **Physical appearance or props**: Darren Tay, the 2016 Toastmasters Champion of Public Speaking, wore a pair of briefs over his pants while delivering his winning speech, "Outsmart; Outlast." He dressed this way to tell the story of how a childhood bully forced him to dress in a similar manner and walk around school. This costume sparks the audience's interest. Seeing him dressed in such a visually enticing way draws the audience in to wonder what it's all about. "What does he want to say dressed like that?" No one wears a pair of briefs over their pants, not even on a runway.

You can also open your speech with props. You can use inanimate objects such as a cigarette like Mohammed Qahtani did in his humorous speech titled, "The Power of Words" which won him the 2015 Toastmasters World Championship of Public Speaking. Or you could use living things like Bill Gates did, releasing live mosquitoes into an audience of hundreds in his 2009 TED talk, titled, "Mosquitoes, Malaria and Education."

- **Silence**: I love the words of Wayne Dyer: "Everything that's created comes out of silence. Thoughts emerge from the nothingness of silence. Words come out of the void. Your very essence emerges from emptiness. All creativity requires some stillness."

These words sum up the power inherent in opening your speech with silence. There is a profound quality that silence can give to your speech. The opening of Aaron Beverly's speech at the 2016 Toastmasters World

Championship of Public Speaking perfectly captured the power of silence. (Aaron came second place in the championship.)

First, Beverly was introduced by the moderator, who read his 57-word speech title out loud. "Live A Lasting Memory Using As Few Words As Possible And Strive With Every Fiber Of Your Being To Avoid Being The Type Of Person Who Rambles On And On With No End In Sight More Likely Than Not Causing More Listeners To Sit And Think To Themselves, 'Oh My Goodness! Can Somebody Please Make This Stop!'"

The title contradicts its message beautifully, and this makes his opening all the more hilarious. The audience, amused by the funny title, laughs and claps as Aaron Beverly makes his way to the stage. When he gets on stage the silence is so deafening you could hear a pin drop. For the next 14 seconds Beverly stares at the audience, expressionless. Then he breaks the silence, and speaks. , "Be honest," he says. You enjoyed that, didn't you?" He smiles. And the laughter in the audience resumes. He's got them all eating out of his hands. And he said barely anything. Anything at all.

- **Body Language**: Sometimes it's good to be a bit more dramatic with your opening. We know that gestures, posture and facial expressions are all important *while* delivering a speech; but what if you decide to start your speech by doing something extra with just your body alone or with your body and your voice? It could be a dance, an imitation, anything at all to attract the attention of your listeners.

The winner of the 2018 Toastmasters World Championship, Ramona J. Smith, used this technique in her speech, "Still Standing." She enters the stage and assumes a boxing stance. With her fists clenched, she says these words: "Life would sometimes feel like a fight. The punches. . ." She throws a punch with her right hand. ". . . jabs. . . " Another punch with her left. ". . . hooks. . ." She demonstrates a hook.

Then stands upright. ". . . will come in the form of challenges, obstacles and failures." She resumes the boxing stance. "Yet, if you stay in the ring and learn from those past fights, at the end of each round . . ." She stands upright. ". . . you'll be still standing."

In this speech, Ramona used her body to convey the power and meaning—and, quite literally the 'punch' behind each word and sentence.

Tip 4: Use pauses often

Selah is a Hebrew word used in musical scores. It is taken to mean a pause or a break. However, its meaning goes deeper than that. Selah means to pause and think deeply; to pause and reflect or contemplate.

Your speech is not a music score, but it is imperative you pause often so that you can allow your message to sink into your audience. A pause is a brief silence. And as I said earlier, silence gives your speech a profound quality. So use pauses to drive home a point. Do not hurry onto the next point when you know there is an idea you *need* your audience to grasp. Pause for few seconds. Your pause may be followed by an applause—an indication that the audience appreciates what you've just said.

As well as giving time to let a message sink in, pause also helps you the speaker to gather your thoughts, as well as prepare the minds of your audience for what you will say next, and this also helps build the suspense.

Also, to use pauses effectively, it is better not to have too *many* long sentences in your speech. Let your sentences be concise and punchy. However, do not sacrifice the rhythm and beauty of your speech on the altar of brevity. Varying the length of your sentences provides the necessary pace and rhythm for your speech, and keeps the audience listening.

There is what is called *ineffective pause*. This pause is not intentional, thus does not add to the effect of the speech. If anything, it distracts the audience. So avoid them at all costs. Filler words are a common example of ineffective pause—"uh," "er," "um," "basically," "y'know," "literally," "actually," "then," "so," etc. Practice your speech as much as possible so that you feel confident; this will help you to avoid the use of filler words. Using ineffective pauses, especially filler words, presents you as an amateur speaker. Imagine reading the transcript of your speech, and the text is filled with "um" and "basically." Wouldn't that turn you off?

Bonus Tip: Lumen Learning advises that you record a speech and count the use of unnecessary pauses and filler words in relation to other words in the speech. Try and reduce the ratio. To add to this, I advise that you keep practicing. The use of filler words is usually a sign of anxiety. Therefore, always practice because practice doesn't only bring perfection, it also fuels confidence.

Tip 5: Connect with your audience by making eye contact

I stumbled on a brief research report on *Inc.* where the writer, Sims Wyeth reveals that in a study carried out at Cornell University, researchers manipulated the gaze of the cartoon rabbit on Trix cereal packages. The result of the study showed that adults were more likely to choose Trix over other cereal brands if the rabbit was looking directly at them. Commenting on the result, Brain Wansink, a professor at Cornell's Dyson School of Applied Economics and Management, said: "Making eye contact, even with a character on a cereal box, inspires powerful feelings of connection."

World-class public speakers do not underestimate the power of eye contact. It is the most important way to connect with your audience. Imagine you are conversing with someone, and the person is looking at something else; you would feel that you have lost their attention, even if they heard everything you said.

Making eye contact with your audience helps you gauge their attention span. If your speech is interesting, you'll see it in their eyes. If it is boring, you'll also see it in their eyes. If you are giving a boring speech, there is also a tendency that you will be unable to make eye contact with majority of your audience, because their eyes will be fixed on something else—maybe their phones, a book, a member of the audience, or in extreme cases, they've fallen asleep.

I wrote earlier that when you deliver a speech, you are constantly interacting with your audience. However, it is not interaction in the normal two-way, verbal communication we are used to, so your audience can only give feedback through their expressions. But, unless you maintain eye contact, how else would you be able to notice these expressions?

Wyeth writes that, by maintaining eye contact, your listeners feel invited to engage with you. They move from bring passive listeners to active ones, signaling their responses to what you are saying through a variety of expressions like frowns, head nods, or raising eye their eyebrows in skepticism.

Bring able to read the expressions of your audience aids your improvisation, or as Wyeth puts it, it helps you respond to the signals of your listeners. Wyeth notes that if your listeners express skepticism, for example, you could say, "I know it seems hard to believe—but I promise you, the investment makes sense. The data bears it out."

We can extract three advantages of maintaining eye from Wyeth's example. One, responding to the audience's expressions gives you something more to say to strengthen your argument. Two, your response may serve as an effective link to your next point. Like in Wyeth's example; after saying "The data bears it out," you could go on to present the data to the audience.

Three, it gives you the chance to address opposing views, thus the audience knows you are not just dumping information on them.

Finally, maintaining eye contact reflects what I call the ABC of your ethos—it reflects your Authority, Believability, and Confidence.

Tip 6: Vary your tone of voice, depending on the impact you are trying to create

In writing, we vary the length of sentences for rhythm and for the reader to appreciate the message being passed. Italics or capitalization can be used for emphasis. But in public speaking, we do not only vary the length of sentence, but also the intonation of our voice. The tone used in one particular statement may not necessarily be the same tone that would be applicable in another.

Your tone can range from being funny, serious, formal, casual, respectful, impolite, authoritative, conversational, to sarcastic, sympathetic, witty, passionate, and so on. If you choose to say something serious with a funny tone, you may only succeed in making the audience laugh without driving home the main message. When it comes to humor, sometimes it is the tone of your words that best conveys its message as humorous, not even relying upon the words themselves. In Chapter Two I talked about the tone in Martin Luther King Jr.'s speech; the *passion* in his voice was palpable each time he said, "I have a dream," imbuing the audience to share in that dream, imploring them to want it, too

The tone of your voice is used to indicate emphasis. When you place a loud, forceful tone on a word or sentence, the audience is alerted to the fact that you consider this information to be important.

How your audience feels as you deliver your speech depends greatly on your tone of voice. So as you invent and rehearse your speech, take into the consideration the tone behind your words. Now, the challenge is you cannot *assess* the tone of your voice because, as Maria Pellicano said, the sound you hear inside your head is quite different from what others are hearing. This is true. Surely there have been times when someone has been offended by what you said, and you didn't know why. In your mind what you think that what you said came off jokingly, while other has felt slighted by your words, interpreting your tone as disrespectful or harsh. So if you can't rightly assess the tone of your voice, how do you know the right tones to use through your speech?

Maria Pellicano offers a simple solution to this: You either record your speech and listen to yourself, or you hire a voice coach. When you listen to yourself andplace yourself in the position of a listener, not a speaker. This way, you can objectively assess what emotion your tone conveys.

Tip 7: Share personal stories that are relevant to your topic and your audience

People love stories. And they love it even more when these stories are nonfictional and personal. People love stories that they can relate to; they love to hear plausible stories. Thus, your speech will resonate more with your listeners when you share personal stories that are *relevant* to your speech.

Nick Vujicic is one of the world's top motivational speakers, and most of his speeches are about himself. Vujucic was born with Tetra-Amelia Syndrome, a very rare congenital disorder, whereby a child is born without arms and legs. At thirty-seven years of age, his speeches offer hope and encouragement, helping people find meaning in life. He talks about how he moved from being in a dark place and contemplating suicide to becoming a more confident and positive man who feels good about himself. With his two small, deformed feet, he operates an electric wheelchair, phone, and computer. He manages to type forty words per minute with his left foot and in good humor brags that, with two cups of coffee, he can increase this word count to fifty-three words.

In Chapter Two, we recounted briefly how Muniba Mazari Baloch used her sad story to inspire, encourage and educate hundreds of people—and the people tuned in to listen to her from their laptops, phones, and televisions.

Your stories may not always be sad; they can be just a simple tale of addressing a life challenge and describing how you overcame it. For instance, in Obama's "Fired Up, Ready to Go" speech, which was delivered at a rally at the University of Maryland in September 2009, he shared the brief story of his campaign for presidency, and how he sought endorsement from a legislative member, even traveling miles to a place called Greenwood. It was a story told to remind us that, in order to get what we want, we must be prepared to go the extra mile (sometimes even literally).

Your personal stories can also be humorous., similar to Dan Pink's speech we looked at earlier. After creating that suspense through the void of silent opening where less turned out to be more, Pink went on to briefly describe his time at law school, and how he had never practiced law in his life. (I have now satisfied your curiosity: now you know the regretful thing that Pink did, and the teaser which worked to get the audience's attention.)

The world's best speakers are authentic and openly share their background, accomplishments and challenges. You can use your personal story to open your speech, or use it in the middle of your speech to buttress a point, or even use it in closing your thoughts, leaving the audience to marinate upon a personal life lesson. In some cases, your entire speech can be centered around your story.

Bonus Tip: Don't just talk about the positive events in your life. Give your audience a glimpse into the adversities, challenges, and problems (including embarrassing situations) you have faced. This will make you more relatable and human to your audience.

Tip 8: Highlight and repeat key points

The aim of highlighting and repeating key points is to solidify your message in the minds of the audience. As you speak, your words are carried away to make space for new information. A listener cannot grasp the entirety of your message, so you need to highlight the important information for them and make them stick. Reiterate your key points and they will not be forgotten.

Another way to use emphasize your key points is by repeating a particular word or phrase for effect. In his "I Have A Dream" speech, Martin Luther King Jr. uses a form of repetition known as anaphora to reiterate the kind of America he desires. He introduces each statement of desire with the words, "I have a dream."

Tip 9: Be expressive with your body language

If you want to have active listeners, you need to be an active speaker. Your speech goes beyond your voice; you have to be expressive with your body. Toastmasters International states that what you are is more clearly communicated through your nonverbal behavior than through your words. Recall the popular saying: "Actions speak louder than words."

The first thing the audience notices about your body language is your *posture*. You cannot be speaking on a message of hope while your body slumps forward in despair. Be relaxed. Stand/sit upright. Don't slouch.

Also, to reiterate: your facial expressions are important. Let your expressions mirror your words. You cannot be sharing a sad story with a smile; neither can you deliver a joke with a straight face, unless it is meant to heighten the effect of the joke.

It is also important to note that, during a speech, the eyes of the audience are more active than their ears. They are watching you—your expressions, your moves—because what they see will help them to better understand your message. Toastmasters notes that your audience use their visual senses to determine whether you are sincere or insincere, confident or insecure, and whether you believe what you are saying, if you are happy and interested to speak to them. So it is important to use *gestures* to demonstrate your point. With gestures you can add more emphasis and support to your words. Generally, in public speaking, there are four types of gestures:

- *Descriptive gestures*: These gestures clarify or enhance what is being said. For instance, using our hands to describe the shape, size, location or other characteristics of a thing or person.
- *Emphatic gestures*: These are used for emphasis. For example, shaking your head as you say the word never in "*Never* allow your challenges keep you down," helps you emphasize the power behind never giving up and never allowing challenges to get the better of you.
- *Suggestive gestures*: These are symbols

of ideas or emotions. In our previous example where shaking your head is an emphatic gesture, it can also be considered a suggestive gesture. By shaking your head, you are indicating your disagreement. Other suggestive gestures include giving a shrug, which suggests ignorance or resignation, or an open palm which suggests giving or receiving.

- *Prompting gestures*: You use these gestures when you want to elicit a response from your audience. For instance, raising your hand as you ask, "Who is happy to be seated here today?" prompts your audience mirror you and do the same.

Toastmasters International sets an important guideline for gestures: Gestures made above the shoulder level suggest physical height, inspiration, or joy. Gestures made below shoulder level indicate rejection, apathy, or condemnation. And those gestures made at or near shoulder level suggest calmness or serenity.

An important point to note is that while gestures are important, you should be careful not to use mannerisms that can distract your audience. You don't see top public speakers pacing, rocking or swaying. They don't lean on the lectern, bite or lick their lips, frown, tap their fingers, adjust their hair or clothes, or in the words of Toastmasters, "[turn] the head and eyes from side to side like an oscillating fan."

Here are a few bonus tips on gestures, culled from Toastmasters International:

- **Respond naturally to what you are saying.** I have always said that as a public speaker, you are your first listener. So as you speak, respond with the gestures that come naturally with your words.
- **Create the conditions for gesturing— not the gesture.** Don't make gestures because you know they are important in public speaking. Doing this will

make your speech mechanical and unnatural. Make gestures because those gestures are appropriate at that time. This is why you need to be totally involved in the invention phase of your speech. Toastmasters writes: "By immersing yourself in your subject matter, you will create the conditions that will enable you to respond naturally with appropriate gestures."

- **Suit the action to the word and the occasion.** Your gestures should be purposeful and reflect your words. The vigor and frequency of the gesture should match the word or statement. Toastmasters makes another valid point that is, when your gesture doesn't match your words, your speech may come across as wooden, artificial, and sometimes comical. Gestures, too, should fit the size and nature of the audience. "The larger the audience, the broader and slower your gestures should be. Also, young audiences are usually attracted to the speaker who uses vigorous gestures, while older, more conservative groups may feel irritated or threatened by a speaker whose physical actions are too powerful."

- **Make your gestures convincing.** "Effective gestures are vigorous enough to be convincing, yet slow enough and broad enough to be clearly visible. Your gestures should be distinct but not jerky, and they should never follow a set pattern."

- **Make your gestures smooth and well-timed.** According to Toastmasters, a gesture has three parts: the *approach*, the *stroke*, and the *return*. During the approach, the body moves in anticipation. The stroke is the gesture itself. The return brings the body back to its original, balanced posture. So a gesture flows in this order: balance

— approach — stroke — return — balance. This flow must be smoothly executed, with only the stroke evident to the audience. Also, this flow must be perfectly timed—the stroke should last *on* the correct word, not before or after it.

Note: Don't try to memorize gestures and insert them into your speech. As stated earlier, they should be natural, smooth, and timely. Toastmasters cautions that memorized gestures often fail because the speaker cues himself or herself by the word the gesture is meant to punctuate, which results in the gesture following the word. The resultant look becomes one that comes across as foolish and artificial.

- **Make natural, spontaneous gesturing a habit**. As a public speaker, don't wait until you are to give a speech before you practice. Take note of your gestures when speaking during normal conversations. Check what you are doing wrong and work on it. That way, gestures flow naturally, whether you are on stage or not.

Always remember that the world's best speakers skilfully use energy, presence, body language, tone variation and pauses to impact the public. This is because effective public speaking is not just about talking—but about taking your audience on a journey.

Tip 10: Use the space on the stage effectively

Stage management is an important quality you must possess as a speaker. I believe this is why Toastmasters World Championship and many TEDx events do not provide lecterns for speakers. They want to see how speakers make use of the space on stage. Your charisma endears you to the audience, and using your space effectively puts your charisma on full display.

But advising you to use your space effectively doesn't mean you should pace round the stage. Relax. Be calm. Just as you own your speech, own your space. Move around whilst maintaining eye contact with the audience. Using all of the area of the stage enhances your communication and connection with the audience. Every member of the audience then feels important, because you care about them enough to reach out to them no matter where they are seated.

However, using your space shouldn't feel forced, unnatural and rehearsed. Let it flow from within you. Remember you are displaying your charisma—a gift you already possess. Use the eye contact you make with the audience to know when to move. If your stage is a raised platform where the audience is seated below, you can even come down and move closer to their level, engaging with them as you would a child, by respectfully going to their level, meeting them eye to eye.

Tip 11: Use an effective close that summarizes the topic and/or provides people with a call to action
End your speech with a bang!

Every part of your speech is important. Some speakers usually do not pay attention to the ending of their speech. They feel it is the end so it doesn't matter.

But that's wrong thinking. Your ending should be as strong as your beginning. It is not enough to have a powerful opening; you should also look to have a compelling close. When the effect of your opening has worn off, your concluding remarks remind your audience about the power in and of your speech and this is what leaves a lasting impression.

In the same way that you shouldn't start your speech with the boring, conventional "Good morning," talk, you shouldn't end your speech with clichéd "Thank You's," either. Be creative with your beginning. Be *very* creative with your ending.

Earlier, I compiled a list of different ways you could use to begin your speech, with examples from renowned speakers. Likewise, I have also compiled a list of ways for closing your speech, also with examples. I extracted these speeches from William Safire's *Lend Me Your Ears: Great Speeches in History*. Here are some ways you could end your speech:

- **Challenge**: You can challenge your audience towards taking action. We see this in Harold Ickes' speech delivered on "I am an American Day," in 1941. Ickes was the Interior Secretary to Franklin Roosevelt. He tackled Americans who questioned America's involvement in the European war. Ickes understood the implications of Adolf Hitler and the Nazi domination, so he delivered a blunt admonition, ending with the words: "We will help brave England drive back the hordes from hell who besiege her, and then we will join for the destruction of savage and bloodthirsty dictators everywhere. But we must be firm and decisive. We must know our will and make it felt. And we must hurry."

- **Quotation**: A speech can be closed with a quote or words of another person. This person can be a speaker or writer, or anyone at all. Provided the quote resonates with you and is in line with your speech and adds strength and weight, then you should close with it, particularly and if you believe it will resonate with the audience as well. Justice Oliver Wendell Holmes, in a tribute on his ninetieth birthday, said: "To live is to function. That is all there is to living. And so I end with a line from a Latin poet who uttered the message more than fifteen hundred years ago: 'Death plucks my ear and says, Live—I am coming.'"

- **Summary**: Your ending should summarize your entire speech. In few, powerful sentences, you tie up everything you've said, rounding out your message in summary. When John D. Rockefeller laid down the guiding principles for his family, he summarized it with these words: "These are the principles upon which alone a new world recognizing the brotherhood of man and the fatherhood of God can be established."

- **Appeal**: Here, you invite the audience to engage in a new line of thought or action. For instance, in his speech defining national greatness, one of the founding fathers of America, Governor Morris, closed his speech with: "I anticipate the day when to command respect in the remotest regions it will be sufficient to say, 'I am an American.' Our flag shall then wave in glory over the ocean and our commerce feel no restraint but what our own government may impose. . . Thank God, to reach this envied state we need only to will. _Yes, my countrymen, our destiny depends on our will. But if we would stand high on the record of time, that will must be inflexible._"

  The underlined sentences in particular demonstrate Morris's invitation for Americans to be resilient in their collective will, in order to reach the desired height/s.

- **Inspiration**: This is similar to the appeal. But unlike appeal where you are arousing the intellect or thoughts of the audience, closing with an inspiration reaches out and touches the *emotions* of the audience. In 1948, Arab forces prepared to attack after Jewish leaders proclaimed Israel a sovereign state. Menachem Begin, an underground fighter, had to pledge the allegiance of his troops to the newborn state. He ended his speech with these inspiring words: "We shall go on our way into battle, soldiers of the Lord of Hosts, inspired by the spirit of our ancient heroes, from the conquerors of Canaan to the Rebels of Judah. . . And in this battle we shall break the enemy and bring salvation to our people, tried in the furnace of persecution, thirsting only for freedom, for righteousness, and for justice."

- **Advice**: Proffering a piece of advice at the end your speech keeps listeners engaged and alert. In 1789, Richard Price, an English cleric, delivered a speech titled, "On the Love of our Country," in support of the French Revolution. In his second to last paragraph, he encouraged the dissenters, whom he called the "friends of freedom." However, his final paragraph was a word of advice—a caution, if you will—to the "oppressors." He said: "You cannot now hold the world in darkness. Struggle no longer against increasing light and liberality. Restore to mankind their rights, and consent to the correction of abuses, before they and you are destroyed together."

- **A solution proposal**: If your speech is centered on a particular problem, you can end the speech by proposing a solution. In his report concerning the tensions between the United States and the Soviet Union, Secretary of State Dean Acheson under the watchful eye of President Harry Truman, ended his talk with this proposal: "The success of our efforts rests finally on our faith in ourselves and in the values for which this Republic stands. We will need courage and steadfastness and the cool heads and steady nerves of citizenry, which has always faced the future 'with malice toward none; with charity toward all; with firmness in the right, as God gives us to see the right.'"

- **Question**: A (rhetorical) question, especially at the end of your speech, gives it a profound quality. You are directly challenging your audience to reflect on a thought. When Architect Frank Lloyd Wright spoke in a meeting of the Association of Federal Architects in 1938, he proposed a new branch of architecture he called

"Organic Architecture." However, he criticized the capacity and effectiveness of the American government to advance American architecture, or his cause. The speech ended with the questions: "What can government do with an advanced idea? If it is still a controversial idea, and any good idea must be so—can government touch it without its eye on at least the next election? It cannot. I know of nothing more silly (*sic*) than to expect 'government' to solve our advanced problems for us. If we have no ideas, how can government have any?"

- **Visualizing the future**: Ending your speech by making projections to what you think the future will be, or considering a probable future event, demonstrates thoughtfulness and a willingness to think futuristically. In 1588, Philip II of Spain, a rejected suitor of Elizabeth I, assembled a fleet of tall ships called the "Invincible Armada." The Queen did not cower in fear; instead, she encouraged her soldiers and inspired them towards victory. She ended her courageous speech by giving them a glimpse of the future: "I know already, by your forwardness, that you have deserved rewards and crowns; and we do assure you, on the word of a prince, they shall be duly paid you. . . not doubting by your obedience to my general, by your concord in the camp, and by your valor in the field, we shall shortly have a famous victory over the enemies of my God, of my kingdom, and of my people."

- **Proverb**: Many proverbs are overused already, so when you want to use a proverb to close your speech, try to use an uncommon one. When, in 532 BC, Eastern Roman Emperor Justinian wanted to flee because he was about to be overthrown and killed by the rebel leader, Hypatius, it was a brief speech by his wife, Empress Theodora, that stopped him, infusing him instead with the courage to kill the rebels. Her final words were: "If you wish to save yourself, my Lord, there is no difficulty. We are rich; over there is the sea, and yonder are the ships. Yet reflect for a moment whether, when you have once escaped to a place of security, you would not gladly exchange such safety for death. As for me, I agree with the adage that the royal purple is the noblest shroud."

Bonus techniques for closing your speech effectively:

- *Prayer*: This is a common technique used by leaders of countries. It is used as a way of praying for the good of the country and her people. When John Hilton, a BBC broadcaster talked about his "calculated spontaneity" as a radio broadcaster, he ended with the three words, "Blessings on you."

- *Invite the audience to say or perform an action*: At the end of your speech you can ask the audience to recite a statement, or perform an action. This is especially useful in motivational speaking, because it helps cement all you've said in the minds of the audience. They will forever remember what was said combined with the action performed, thus, remembering your speech. In 1945, the presiding judge of the Second Circuit Court of Appeals from 1939 to 1951, Judge Learned Hand, gave a speech during an "I am an American Day," where he spoke on the need to uphold the spirit of liberty. These were his closing words: "In confidence that you share that belief, I now ask you to raise your hands and repeat with me this pledge: *I pledge allegiance to the flag of the United States of America, and to the Republic for which it stands—one nation indivisible, with liberty and justice for all."*

- *Repetition*: Just as repetition is effective in the beginning and middle of a speech, so too is it an effective tool to use at the end. Repeating a particular word or a phrase or a sentence drives home the message you want to deliver through your speech. President Calvin Coolidge affirmed his faith in Massachusetts when he took the chair of the state's senate and ended his address thus: "Let the laws of Massachusetts proclaim to her humblest citizen, performing the most menial task, the *recognition* of his manhood, the *recognition* that all men are peers, the humblest with the most exalted, the *recognition* that all work is glorified. *Such* is the path to equality before the law. *Such* is the foundation of liberty under the law. *Such* is the sublime revelation of man's relation to man—democracy." (The emphasis here of course, is mine.)

- *Thank You*: I know I said earlier that you shouldn't use the mundane close of "Thank You." But you can use it—only if you can be creative with it the way Mark Twain was in his 1906 speech, in which he recounted his first public appearance and the stage fright that followed. The speech was made at his daughter's singing debut as a contralto in Norfolk, Connecticut. Twain didn't thank his audience for listening to his speech, but for something else. He said: "But I shall never forget my feelings before the agony left me, and I got up here to thank you for her for helping my daughter, by your kindness, to live through her first appearance. And I want to thank you for your appreciation of her singing, which is, by the way, hereditary."

So here are my tips on public speaking and I believe you will find them useful. Before I wrap up this chapter, I would like to present an exposition on two of the greatest speakers the world has ever seen, because I believe that many of the leading public speakers we know of today were truly inspired by these men.

A Tale of Two Speakers:
Abraham Lincoln[1] and Winston Churchill

Abraham Lincoln. Winston Churchill. Two politicians—one born nine years after the death of the other—who used their words to implant new narratives in the minds of their countrymen. Their lives as public speakers hold vital lessons for all of us. Although they were not always perfect speakers in the early stages of their lives, they both went on to become two of the greatest models for public speaking the world has ever known. Their physical appearance, use of voice, mannerisms, speeches, and preparations have all been used as instructional materials, both for

1. Commentaries on Abraham Lincoln's life as a public speaker were culled from *Abraham Lincoln Online. Speeches & Writings.* **www.abrahamlincolnonline.org/ lincoln/speeches/speaker.htm.** Accessed 22 July 2020.

speakers who were their contemporaries and for the speakers that have followed. Let's examine the lives of Abraham Lincoln and Winston Churchill as public speakers.

Appearance

A picture of Abraham Lincoln reveals the portrait of an ungainly and lanky fellow. His cheekbones jut out of his face, carving themselves inwards as they come to join his upper lip. Lincoln is easily recognizable by the tufts of beard that covers his jaw.

At six feet four inches, Lincoln was very tall. A tall appearance usually comes with an air of grace and greatness; it commands authority and reverence. But this was not so for the 16th President of the United States, whose appearance Abram Bergen described as "uncouth" and "awkward." In talking about one of Lincoln's speeches, William H. Herndon—a law partner and biographer of Abraham Lincoln—said it seemed as though Lincoln's general look, from his pose, form, momentary bouts of shyness, even the color of his flesh, which was considered"wrinkled and dry," all seemed to be stacked against him, before even beginning of his speech.

If you've read the story of Abraham Lincoln, you will know that he was a man who faced a lot of challenges in his life. Maybe that was why Joshua Speed describes Lincoln as a sad man; a sadness seen most of the time on his countenance. The *Daily Advertiser* in 1848 described him as a figure with an "intellectual face, showing a searching mind, and a cool judgment." Despite his sad countenance, Speed noted that once Lincoln got on stage he immediately warmed up; "his face was radiant and glowing, and almost gave expression to his thoughts before his tongue would utter them."

I believe Lincoln knew of his strengths and weaknesses. He knew that his physical appearance didn't do him any justice so he had to rely on presenting a pleasant face first, as a way of gaining acceptance before he delivered his words. Lincoln understood the effect one wrong facial expression could have on his audience. He didn't have an appealing physical appearance anyway, but that didn't matter; so long as he could present a pleasant face to his audience.

With his one-piece suit, hat, and cigar stuck to his

lips, Winston Churchill, on the other hand, looked like a leader of a mafia—a godfather. His appearance was in perfect contrast to that of the more reserved Abraham Lincoln. Although he was only five feet seven inches tall, Churchill's dress sense made him an imposing figure and endeared him to the public, just as he was often portrayed in photographs and cartoons. His appearance became his signature, his identity. His chubby face was pleasant and handsome when he smiled, and grave and intimidating when he frowned, and he knew exactly the right moment to transition from one to the other.

Lesson 1: Know your strong points and weak points. Present your strong points first to your audience. You may not get a second chance to make a first impression, so do all you have to do at the beginning. Win the hearts of your audience immediately. If you know your appearance places you at a disadvantage, start your speech with a strong opening that resonates. You can even use a comment on your appearance to create laughter, which will relax you as well as the audience;

think of it as a deliberate ice breaker, based on the fact that the audience may have already formed opinions about you based on your appearance, and use it to your advantage.

Also, have a good dress sense. What you lack in physique you can gain with fashion. As a speaker, learn to dress well. Be smart and neat. Your clothes must not be sophisticated, they can still be simple, yet classy. Don't look shabby. Whether you want to go casual with a tee-shirt and a pair of denim jeans like Steve Jobs, or if you want the corporate look like Arnold Schwarzenegger, make sure you come out with a touch of style and class. People should remember you only by your words, but it is also to your advantage if they remember you by your looks.

Voice

Lincoln had an unpleasant voice. In a letter written in 1887, William H. Herndon described Lincoln's voice as "shrill, squeaking, piping, unpleasant." But his voice didn't stop him from spellbinding his audience. About Lincoln's second inaugural address, Noah Brooks writes: "The address was received in most profound silence. Every word was *clear* and *audible* as the ringing and somewhat shrill tones of Lincoln's voice sounded over the vast concourse."

Churchill's voice however, was not as appealing nor as commanding as his appearance. His voice was raspy; it sounded like the caw of a crow. The one good thing about this vocal quality is that it is loud, albeit grating. Maybe this was why Churchill hated the microphone. Quoting Harold Nicolson, Kristin Hunt states in an article from *Smithsonian Magazine* that Churchill not only hated the microphone but "sounded ghastly on the wireless."

Listening to Churchill speak, one cannot help but notice his lisp—and his obvious struggle to pronounce "s" and "z" sounds. But this didn't stop Churchill from speaking. In an exposition on Churchill's speech impediment, John Mather writes that, "Churchill persevered as he worked on his pronunciation. He undertook a pronunciation exercise with phrases such as 'The Spanish ships I cannot see for they are not in sight.'" This exercise was intended to cure his problem with pronouncing the "s" sound. After a well-received political speech, Churchill himself proclaimed that he would indeed become a great speaker, saying, "My impediment is no hindrance." And indeed it was not.

Besides of his impeccable fashion style, Churchill made up for his speech impediment with the content of his speech and unique mannerisms.

Lesson 2: You don't choose your voice. It is a part of you that you cannot control or change. However, you can work on it. Lincoln's voice was shrill and unpleasant, but he never failed to make his speech lucid and audible. He enunciated his words. Churchill, on the other hand, made sure he worked on his lisp and also tried to pronounce his words clearly so he could be understood.

You need not worry if you feel your voice isn't pleasant enough. Just deliver your words clearly and with the right pace and rhythm. The audience may not appreciate your voice; however they know that you have no control over it, and it won't be long before they channel their entire focus onto your words—provided you give them a reason to.

Mannerisms

Before a speech, Lincoln usually appeared shy and awkward. Two different men at different times wrote notably similar narratives about Lincoln's mannerisms before a speech. Robert B. Rutledge wrote in an 1866 letter that when Lincoln made his first attempt at public speaking in a debating club of which Rutledge was President at the time, he thrust his two hands "down deep in the pockets of his pantaloons." In a similar description written eleven years later, William H. Herndon, in 1887, said that when Lincoln rose to address an audience, he would place "his hands behind him, the back part of his left hand resting in the palm of his right hand."

However, as his speech progressed, Lincoln usually eased into the activity and became freer in his movements and gestures. Rutledge wrote that as Lincoln "warmed with his subject, his hands would forsake his pockets and [instead] enforce his ideas by awkward gestures." Similarly, Herndon recounted that as Lincoln "proceeded and grew warmer, he moved his hands to the front of his person, generally interlocking his fingers and running one thumb around the other."

What is most interesting about Lincoln's mannerisms were his gestures. Recall that I said since his appearance and voice put him at a disadvantage, Lincoln had learned instead to use his strengths to drive home his message. And his gestures were one of his strong points. Of his gestures, Herndon wrote: ". . . he used his hands—especially and generally his right hand—in his gestures; he used his head a great deal in speaking, throwing or jerking or moving it now here and now there, now in this position and now in that, in order to be more emphatic, to drive the idea home. Mr. Lincoln never beat the air, never sawed space with his hands, never acted for stage effect . . . he spoke and acted to convince individuals and masses; he used in his gestures his right hand, sometimes shooting out that long bony forefinger of his to dot an idea or to express a thought, resting his thumb on his middle finger. <u>Bear in mind that he did not gesticulate much and yet *it is true* that every organ of his body was in motion and acted with ease, elegance, and grace</u> . . ."

Winston Churchill, on the other hand, had what

many described as "upper-class mannerisms." This came from being highborn and highbrow. In an article describing Churchill's style, *Canadian Business* states that he often "stood squarely, usually with one hand grasping his lapel or resting firmly on his hip. His other arm occasionally came forward to make a strong vertical gesture to emphasize a point he was making." The article further notes that Churchill made sure he never rotated his arms round his body, as that would "undercut his strength and dignity as a speaker."

Quoting William Manchester's biography of Winston Churchill titled, *The Last Lion*, critic and philosopher, William Hazlitt states that, "Splendid prose. . . should be accompanied by vehemence and gesture, a dramatic tone, flashing eyes and 'conscious attitude'—a precise description of Churchillian delivery.'" (Gary Genard, n.d.)

One signature feature of Churchill's speeches for which he was well known was the dramatic pause, which he liked to use for emphasis. And it was always effective. Thomas Montalbo quotes Churchill to have said that "he once made a pause to allow the House to take it in . . . As this soaked in, there was something like a gasp." Montalbo notes that Churchill relied on timing too, for heightened effect, because "it made silence even more eloquent than words," thus allowing his listeners to assimilate to what they had heard, prepare for what would come next. According to Montalbo, Churchill's pauses "forced any restless members of his audience to look at him and listen. He was such a master of pauses that even his throat clearings came at the appropriate moments."

Lesson 3: While I recommend that you show confidence from the start to the end of your speech like Winston Churchill, I will not ignore the fact that, depending on the event, you may feel quite nervous. But learn from Lincoln: you can start nervously; just never end nervously. Ensure that you become relaxed within the first few minutes of your speech. Allow your words to flow out of you. Dispel every tension. Use gestures effectively. I underlined part of Herndon's aforementioned narration to reiterate that your gestures be natural. They should never be forced.

Speeches

Lincoln's speeches can be described with one word: powerful. His speeches were logical, clear, easily comprehensible, and filled with wisdom. His major method of persuasion was logos, then pathos. In his lifetime, many media houses have made glowing remarks about his speeches. The *Daily Journal* of September 18, 1848 described one of Lincoln's speeches as "replete with good sense, sound reasoning, and irresistible argument." Commenting on another speech made eight years later, the *Democratic Press* of July 21, 1856 described Lincoln as "calm, clear and forcible, constantly referring to indisputable facts in our political history..." The *Pantagraph* of September 3, 1858 wondered, "how any reasonable man can hear one of Mr. Lincoln's speeches without being converted to Republicanism."

Lincoln's robust speeches touched every salient aspect of the subject matter; this he was able to do because he gave himself to understanding and comprehension. He studied and placed himself side by side with others—analyzing what they lacked, and what he had. William H. Herndon In an 1865 lecture,

William H. Herndon said that Lincoln "had a good understanding—he had that faculty that knows and comprehends things in their relations." Twelve years later, Herndon would go on describe Lincoln as "cool, careful, earnest, sincere, truthful, fair, self-possessed, not insulting, not dictatorial. A man who was clear in his ideas, simple in his words, strong, terse, and demonstrative."

Winston Churchill was renowned for his speeches during the Second World War. His strong will and stubbornness as an individual was also felt in his speeches. He aimed to empower and motivate. Little wonder in 1989 he said: "I do not care so much for the principles I advocate, as for the impression which my words produce and the reputation they give me."[2]

In a commentary about Churchill's oratory style, Brett & Kate McKay write that Churchill disliked "unnecessarily long and flowery words . . . bureaucratic jargon and toothless euphemisms." His words were

---

2. Sarah H. Howells. "Churchill, Leadership and the War (2) — The Leader as Communicator." *Finest Hour 158, Spring 2013.* **https://winstonchurchill.org/publications/finest-hour/finest-hour-158/churchill-leadership-and-the-war-2-the-leader-as-communicator/**. Accessed 23 July 2020.

mainly short and direct—a quality that set him apart from other politicians. Brett & Kate also note that he used terms like "the poor" and "homes," where other politicians merely referred to such economic statuses as "the lower income group" and "accommodation units."

Furthermore, Churchill's speeches had a rhythmical essence to them. Brett & Kate write that they "had a compelling cadence and rhythm — an almost musical quality." Churchill was also a master of literature. He *intentionally* wove literary devices into his speeches. He employed repetition to heighten emotions, too. For example, in his popular "We shall fight on the beaches!" speech, he purportedly said: "We shall go on to the end, we shall fight in France, we shall fight on the seas and oceans, we shall fight with growing confidence and growing strength in the air, we shall defend our island, whatever the cost may be, we shall fight on the beaches, we shall fight on the landing grounds, we shall fight in the fields and in the streets, we shall never surrender." The repetition here drives home Churchill's resolve to fight, and his efforts to instill such message in his people. Another rare literary technique used was chiasmus; that is, inverting the relationship between elements of phrases in his speech. Brett & Kate wrote that, in 1942, after the first major victory in the war at El Alamein, Churchill had said: "Now this is not the end. It is not even the beginning of the end. But it is, perhaps, the end of the beginning." Churchill's biographer, William Manchester, noted that the Prime Minister loved the effect of gathering "his adjectives in squads of four." He described Bernard Montgomery, a senior British Army officer, as "austere, severe, accomplished, tireless"; and Joseph Chamberlain, a British statesman, as "lively, sparkling, insurgent, compulsive."

Churchill famously was a fan of powerful endings. In his 1897 essay, "The Scaffolding of Rhetoric," he described what he called the "accumulation of argument." He believed that the climax of a speech should provide sound and vivid pictures to the audience, and that all the facts in the speech should point to the climax. When this is done right, the enthusiasm of the audience rises in anticipation of the conclusion.

In his speeches, Churchill placed the most important points at the beginning and repeated them throughout the speech in myriad ways. Brett & Kate note that Churchill advised speakers, thus: "If you have an important point to make, don't try to be subtle or clever. Use a pile driver. Hit the point once. Then come back and hit it again. Then hit it a third time — with a tremendous whack."

Churchill adorned his speeches with vivid analogies and imageries. With such imageries, "his words became more real than the scenes depicted, and more evocative than the sum of his grammatical strokes and rhetorical shadings," wrote Manchester. Churchill referred to the Germans as "carnivorous sheep," and Hitler as a "bloodthirsty guttersnipe." Such analogies and imageries were sometimes peppered with wit and humor; like when Churchill remarked about the growing threat of the Nazis, saying: "A baboon in a forest is a matter of legitimate speculation; a baboon in a zoo is an object of public curiosity; but a baboon in your wife's bed is a cause of the gravest concern."

Winston Churchill used literary qualities in his speeches with one primary aim in mind: to echo the sentiments of his countrymen. He was the voice of the people. Manchester wrote that Churchill spoke *for* his fellow Englishmen, not *to* them. It is for this reason I believe, that while already leaning on his ethos as Prime Minister, Churchill employed pathos as his major means of persuasion. He didn't need to persuade the people as much with logic, since he was confident that the people already saw the logical dynamics of the situation on the ground.

It cannot be argued that Churchill was the most emotionally invested in his speeches. Being a martial man, he was intrigued by, as Brett & Kate put it, the "excitement and sorrow, danger and meaning" of the heroism needed in war. They note that when Churchill dictated his speeches, "his emotion was so raw and real that sometimes he and his secretary would both be crying." No wonder he was able to evoke similar emotions in his listeners. This confirms my earlier assertion that as a speaker, *you* are your first audience; you must first feel the emotions you want your audience to feel. English author, Victoria Sackville-West who listened to Churchill's "We shall fight on the beaches" speech said that the speech "sent shivers (not of fear)" down her spine. She went on to say that his words had a "massive backing of power and resolve behind them, like a great fortress: they are never words for word's sake."

Lesson 4: These two men show the effectiveness of different styles of public speaking. Abraham Lincoln knew how to captivate with his logic and proofs. Using mainly inartistic proofs, he roused the emotions of his audience and introduced a new line of thought. Slavery was a law in Lincoln's time; and since he disapproved of the practice, he had to use his oratory prowess to persuade others to shy away from the practice. William Churchill, on the other hand, was a master of literature and emotions. He used mainly artistic proofs in his speeches. The most important lessons we learn from Churchill were that his speeches inspired him as much as they did his audience.

Since we have seen the effectiveness of these two styles, imagine the power that a blend of these styles would have in the minds of listeners;, even more beauty, even more permanence. Even as separate speeches, both Lincoln and

Churchill's talents in the public speaking arena were both standout performances, and extraordinary in their own right.

Preparation

Every venture in life requires adequate preparation, and Lincoln was never found wanting in this area. He always prepared for his speeches; and for a man who delivered a lot of speeches during his lifetime, one has to wonder at the intensity of his preparations. William H. Herndon, in another lecture in 1866, sheds insight into Lincoln's preparation. He said: "Mr. Lincoln thought his speeches out on his feet, walking in the streets: he penned them in small scraps—sentences, and paragraphs, depositing them in his hat for safety. When fully finished, he would recopy, and could always repeat easily by heart—so well thought out, shotted (*sic*), and matured were they."

If Winston Churchill ever thought he could perform a speech without practicing, his speech impediment always made him rethink his decision.

Churchill often paced around his office or home,

rehearsing lines. He had shorthand secretaries who took down his words and had them typed out for further review. He was never hasty, either, in crafting his speeches; he took great care to choose and craft his words which had been dictated beforehand, and which had been meticulously revised and polished.3 Corroborating this, Brett & Kate state that a single 40-minute speech would take about six to eight hours for Churchill to write, and be subject to numerous revisions.

More revealing still was that Churchill wrote out his speeches in a "psalm form" to aid his delivery. He was so detailed that he would indicate at which junctures he would pause, or where he expected an ovation during his speech; which words or letter to emphasize, and even where he'd appear "to stumble a bit, grope for a word, and 'correct' himself." Brett & Kate comment that, "Churchill knew that a flawless, robotic recital would put people to sleep, and that the more naturalistic a speech seemed, the more attuned

3 Sarah H. Howells. "Churchill, Leadership and the War (2) — The Leader as Communicator." *Finest Hour 158, Spring 2013.* **https://winstonchurchill.org/publications/finest-hour/finest-hour-158/churchill-leadership-and-the-war-2-the-leader-as-communicator/**. Accessed 23 July 2020.

his audience would be." So he prepared for *everything*—every moment, every sentence, every word.

Churchill loved words; and he learnt new words. He broadened his mind and vocabulary with books. According to Brett & Kate, Churchill's vocabulary has been estimated to contain about 65,000 words; this is more than twice that of an average person's library of 25,000. And when he didn't find the right word that could expressly communicate what he had in mind, Churchill invented his own word. Words like "summit," "Middle East," and "iron curtain" are al accredited to him. And he read over 5,000 books spanning diverse genres—immersing himself in everything, from poetry to history to science fiction.

> *Lesson 5: The preparatory activities of Lincoln and Churchill, especially the latter, shows us that public speaking is serious business and to treat it as such. Don't expect to be an excellent speaker when you don't give time to adequate preparation. You might say, "Ron, I have seen people deliver excellent impromptu speeches. They did well even without preparation." This*

is totally false! People who give impromptu speeches have always prepared and practiced for that moment. They know that one day they might be called up to speak without prior notice, so they plan and prepare well ahead of time. Mark Twain wrote his impromptu speeches a week before the event he was to attend. The world's best speakers understand the business of public speaking, and they give it the respect it deserves—to treat it as a profession, not just a hobby.

The best speakers in the world are also great readers and writers. Speaking and writing go hand in hand, as we have just seen with Lincoln and Churchill. So read and write as much as you can. It will dramatically help you expand your vocabulary and grammar skills. It will also improve your perspective, which in turn will allow you to form better speeches and assist you as you become a better speaker.

Give time to preparation. Churchill put so much effort into preparing his speeches because he didn't want to be like the kind of speakers *he detested—speakers that, "before they get up, do not know what they are going to say; and, when they are speaking, do not know what they are saying; and when they have sat down, do not know what they have said." Do not be that speaker. Be intentional about your development. Never fail to practice. Never fail to prepare.*

CHAPTER FOUR

Some of The World's Top Public Speakers in Recent Times

"Don't ever speak publicly about anything you're not passionate about and that you don't actually believe you have something truly unique to deliver."

TONY ROBBINS

So far in this book I have examined the public speaking lives of historical figures—from Aristotle and Cicero, to Abraham Lincoln and Winston Churchill. Although I cited several examples along with our contemporary speakers, in this chapter I will be doing a brief exposition of some of these present-day speakers..

They all have their individual uniqueness and style, and we will see how their various techniques have been adapted from past public speakers, to be passed down through the ages.

All of the world's current leading public speakers embody the fact that, to be a great speaker, you have to understand and apply the principles of public speaking and infuse your creativity into the mix. Just like Aristotle and Abraham Lincoln left their audiences spellbound back in the day, public speakers in the world today continue to intrigue and empower their listeners—and in many cases, the world—with their speeches. They show us that words are ever golden, ever powerful, ever capable of transforming lives and shaping the world for the better.

There are a lot of excellent public speakers in the world today. I could write endlessly about all of them; but if I did, you would probably end up exhausted by the weight of this book. So I will spare you—and myself—that task by looking at just a few of the world's top public speakers.

Tony Robbins

Business Insider describes him as an "electric public speaker," though he is also a motivational speaker, author and coach who is famous for his infomercials, self-help books and his 2006 TED talk in in Monterey, California, titled, *"Why We Do The Things We Do."* Tony Robbins is an energetic 60-year old with the face and body of an athlete; he holds multiple seminars annually around the themes of "self-help" and "positive thinking." His seminars include *Unleash the Power Within*, *Date with Destiny*, *Life and Wealth Mastery*, and *Leadership Academy*.

Robbins is an interactive speaker and loves to engage his audience with questions, which they respond to either by a gesture such as raising their hands or verbally shouting out the answers. Robbins never fails to tell stories, especially personal stories— one of the most popular of being how he started out as a poor janitor with a troubled childhood, tobecaming a famous life coach and public speaker by the time he hit his mid-20s. His stories are effervescent and inspirational, and never fail to spark the 'can-do' spirit in his audience.

Paid up to $300,000 for a speech, Robbins carries his audience along on a journey through his speeches; he outlines his points, reminds the audience of these points at specific moments as he speaks, then summarizes all of his points at the end. He peppers his speeches with bursts of humor, using it as a way to drive home a point or relax his audience.

Tony's gestures are decisive and undramatic. He ensures he doesn't distract his audience with any unnecessary movements, so even though he moves back and forth on stage, he never strays too far from the center. He comes off as a super friendly American, part jock, part boy-next-door, and his style is both unassuming, approachable and down-to-earth. In his public speaking engagements he employs many interactive techniques, known to often leave the stage to high-five a member of the audience.

With his button down shirt and sports jacket, Robbins never comes across as too formal. His fashion style, coupled with his mannerisms, makes his audience more comfortable and relaxed, willing to interact with him, and at this he excels.

Dan Pink

Dan Pink loves to open his speeches with an element of suspense. The American author, (who still regrets having gone to law school), has four of his books listed as New York Times bestsellers. He was the chief speechwriter for Vice President, Al Gore from 1995 to 1997, and his TED talk, *"The Puzzle of Motivation,"* (which he delivered in 2009) has been viewed over 25 million times. (Actually 25,999,776 at this time of writing.)

Pink is a master storyteller and performer who uses strong hand gestures to emphasize and illustrate his points. He advises public speakers to find and hone their unique styles. He told Drake Baer of the *Business Insider* in 2014: ". . . you don't want to sound like Ken Robinson. And you don't want to sound like Tony Robbins. You want to sound like the first *you*, that's going to be much better. So sound like yourself." To sound like yourself, Pink suggests you use a tape recorder, grab a beer with a friend or spouse, partner or loved one—and have them ask you questions about your topic. "Just answer the questions like you would when talking to somebody. That's going to give you the building blocks for sounding like yourself," he said.

Indira Gandhi

While she is known as the first and only female Prime Minister of India, Indira is also remembered for her eloquence and oratorical skills. Her speeches, which focused on social ills like marginalization and oppression, were substantiated with stories of her childhood. Fearlessly she spoke against those at the top of the socioeconomic ladder. Badri Narayan writes that, "her oratory, replete with phrases such as *garibi hatao* (eradicate poverty) and *Harijan dahan* (burning of dalit villages), was designed to provoke social jealousies against the dominant classes and made her very popular."

Some of her famous speeches include her speech on Martin Luther King Jr., delivered in 1969, and *"What Educated Women Can Do"* delivered in 1974 at the Golden Jubilee Celebrations of The Indraprastha College For Women, New Delhi, India.

Margaret Thatcher

Just like her Indian contemporary, Margaret was the first (but not the only) female Prime Minister of the UK. Dubbed "The Iron Lady" for her uncompromising and tough policies, Margaret Thatcher was a great speaker. Her firmness wasn't only demonstrated by her decisions and actions, but also in her voice. She delivered her speeches with the utmost confidence and authority.

Margaret's tone of voice failed to have the emotional quality that her speeches should have contained. It was for this reason that television producer, Gordon Reece advised her to make her deliveries "more intimate" by lowering the tone of her voice, speaking more slowly, and moving closer to the microphone. To do this (and also to remove the strain of her voice), she often drank warm water flavored with honey and lemon. (Realbusiness.co.uk).

Public speaking became her passion and turned into her career after leaving office in 1990. In a 2002 article in *The Guardian*, Julian Glover reveals that she earned up to $50,000 for each speech. Sadly, after suffering a series of strokes, Margaret was forced to retire from public speaking in 2002 upon the advisement of her doctors.

Eric Thomas

Also known as "ET The Hip-Hop Preacher," Eric is an eccentric, energetic, and highly charismatic motivational speaker with a stern countenance. Mostly dressed in a tee-shirt and face cap, Thomas has the persona of a no-nonsense basketball coach. As a matter of fact, ESPN's Eric Woodyard says that Thomas has become a "go-to source of inspiration for NBA players." His words are like a torch—the audience grows "uncomfortable" by the heat he produces, soon becoming on fire themselves, burning passionately all because Thomas roused something in them. Little wonder that the Cleveland Cavaliers' power forward, Andre Drummond, called him "a ball of light."

Averaging 120 – 200 speeches per year, Woodyard says that Thomas has worked with many professional sports teams including the LA Clippers, Milwaukee Bucks, Cleveland Cavaliers, and Atlanta Hawks. Thomas uses real life experiences to connect with his audience and motivate them, and doesn't need his audience to be physically present before he motivates them into action; today, his social media pages are also his stage, and he posts motivational messages to over 1.5 million Instagram followers and over 435,000 Twitter followers daily.

He is raw. He is real. He is irregular. And that's what makes him Eric Thomas.

Mohammed Qahtani

The Saudi Arabian security engineer is a new entrant onto the public speaking scene. Qahtani gained popularity when he won the 2015 Toastmasters World Championship for Public Speaking. In the finals, Qahtani delivered a brilliant, unpredictable speech titled, *"The Power of Words."* He began the speech defending the tobacco industry and using facts that his listeners were ignorant of. And they were ignorant of these facts because, as they would soon learn, all of the facts were false and had beenfabricated by Qahtani. It was this ingenuity—this clever exhibition of how words can be used to sway and persuade as long as they are delivered properly—that earned Qahtani this most deserving win.

The popular themes in Qahtani's speeches include making dreams reality, overcoming fears, goal planning, coping with changes, building the perfect team, and how to captivate an audience with a memorable speech.

Qahtani is also a great storyteller. In *"The Power of Words,"* he shared various stories which revolved around this theme, the power of words. It is interesting to note that he grew up with a stutter,; but as we know by now, a stutter didn't stop him. Also passionate about stand-up comedy, Qahtani has learned to focus on his strength—humor—as a way of overcoming his weakness. Richard Feloni writes that Qahtani accepts that his vocal delivery or stage presence will never be his strongest points, so he heeds the advice of a fellow Toastmasters member who said to him: "Some people are strong with their words. Some people are strong with their voice. Some people are strong with their stage presence. Your strength is humor. Use it."

Mother Theresa

We often remember the nun Mother Theresa with multiple citizenships—Indian, Ottoman, Yugoslavian,

American—and as a symbol of compassion, love and peace; lesser known was the fact that she was a great public speaker, too. Although the subject of controversy, Mother Teresa never stopped speaking on things she was passionate about—love, poverty, giving to others and caring for the poor. This points to the fact that she employed pathos as her major means of persuasion.

Mother Theresa's voice wasn't brittle even in old age. She delivered her speeches with a clear voice and in a *plain* language. In her thesis, "Give Until It Hurts: The Speeches and Letters of Mother Teresa," Veronica Juarez notes that Mother Teresa's speeches were often criticized and/or left unexamined because they had "rhetorical inadequacies." Analyzing four of Mother Teresa's speeches, Juarez realizes that, "within the simplicity of her discourse lies a multifaceted way of expressing her complex faith to an array of audiences."

Mother Theresa deviated from the principles of public speaking but she never deviated from her message—and in this way she consistently stirred the minds of her listeners towards positive thinking and action. Her public speaking style may not be used as instructional material for public speaking today; but if you love her style and want to adopt her methods, remember these words of Veronica Juarez: "Unadorned language, *together with credibility*, is powerful."

Barack Obama

I have mentioned the immediate past President of the United States a lot in this book because to me he epitomizes quality oratory and flawless speech delivery. I consider him a perfect blend of Lincoln and Churchill, and his love for literature can be heard in the singsong quality of his sentences.

When Obama was about to leave office, many confessed that what they would miss most about him were his speeches. Obama was a speaker who knew his audience, and knew how to enrapture them with his words and voice. Many of his speeches are often laden with personal stories; he didn't just address the audience physically present with him—he made sure to tell others watching and listening in their homes in any part of the world that he was talking to them, too.

Obama's voice is clear. His words are measured, not rushed. And he uses pause methods effectively.

Obama is a dynamic speaker whose speeches transition from one mood to another in order to evoke the desired emotions in his audience. His speeches range from being motivational, to humorous, solemn, or even intimate, depending on the message he is trying to imbue.

Some of Obama's most memorable speeches include his acceptance speech at the Democratic National Convention in August 2008; his address and eulogy in Charleston in June 2015 in relation to a mass shooting; his second inaugural address in January 2013; his civil rights march anniversary speech in March 2015, and his anniversary speech which he delivered in January 2016 and which revisited the tragic events of the Sandy Hook Elementary School shooting.

Michelle Obama

The world doesn't often hear the voice of First Ladies, but this wasn't so for "The Girl of the Southside" who has become a remarkable speaker in her own right, much like her husband. Catherine McGrath states that Michelle Obama became a world-class speaker because she wanted "to make an impact on issues important to her. She didn't want to be an invisible First Lady." According to McGrath, Michelle used the resources of the White House, the U.S. Democratic Party and the Obama campaign to nurture and grow herself as public speaker.

Buffalo7.co.uk, in recounting the public speaking journey of the then first lady, recalls that Michelle appeared nervous during Barack's campaign in 2008. She stumbled over her sentences, repeated sentences to correct her mistakes, spoke slowly and used hand gestures in a manner that seemed unnatural and excessive. Eight years later at the 2016 National Democratic Convention, Michelle's delivery was in stark contrast to what the public had seen in 2008; she was calm, her body language was controlled, and there was an effective use of pauses.

An interesting thing about Michelle is that aside campaigning for her husband, she didn't dabble in politics or governance with her speeches. Her speeches are often riddled with stories, especially about her childhood, her children, and her motherhood experiences, which she uses to convey emotions and logic. In eight years, Michelle grew from a novice, timid public speaker to a confident one whose speaking fee, according to buffalo7.co.uk, was estimated to be at $200,000 per speech as at the end of her time as FLOTUS in 2017. She has become a passionate speaker on female empowerment, black empowerment, women's rights issues and other social issues—in this way showing us all how important it is to speak to what one is passionate about, and to keep on speaking about one's passions.

CONCLUSION

It is my hope that you will apply the lessons you have learned in this book to develop your public speaking skills. Always be eager to learn. Hang around people who are also passionate about public speaking.

Never allow fear to get the better of you. Do not shy away from public speaking opportunities. If you feel you want to compete in the next Toastmasters World Championship, then go for it. Never limit yourself.

It is my expectation that when next the names of the top public speakers are listed, your name will be here on this list, because this book has shown you how to speak like the world's top public speakers.

Addendum

Hey, guess what? Remember that girl back at the beginning, Amy, the Valedictorian? Well, those five minutes didn't turn out to be the most embarrassing moments of her life, after all. She delivered her valedictory speech perfectly. Her friends, professors, and family were all impressed by her performance. "Where did you learn to speak so well?" They all asked. She smiled as she remembered the time and effort she put into practicing, into overcoming her fears, into ensuring that her audience were inspired by her words. And she was grateful that her hard work was rewarded.

I want this to be your story, too.

NOTES

Theo Tsaousides. "Why Are We Scared of Public Speaking?" *Psychology Today*, 27 November 2017.

Brett & Kate McKay. "Classical Rhetoric 101: A Brief History." *Art of Manliness*, 30 November 2010. **www.artofmanliness. com/articles/history-of-rhetoric/**. Accessed 5 July 2020.

Peter A. Decaro. "Chapter 2: Origins of Public Speaking." *The Public Speaking Project*. Provided by: University of Alaska, Fairbanks, AK.

Mark Cartwright. "Ancient Greek Government." *Ancient History Encyclopedia*, 20 March 2018. **www.ancient.eu/Greek Government/.** Accessed 5 July 2020.

George Briscoe Kerferd. "Sophist." *Britannica*. **www.britannica. com/topic/Sophist-philosophy**. Accessed 5 July 2020.

Stanford Encyclopedia of Philosophy. "The Sophists." *Stanford Encyclopedia of Philosophy*, 30 September 2011. **www.plato.stanford.edu/entries/sophists/**. Accessed 5 July 2020.

Matthew Dillon & Lynda Garland. *Ancient Rome: From the Early Republic to the Assassination of Julius Caesar*. Taylor & Francis, 2005.

John P. V. Dacre Balsdon. "Marcus Tullius Cicero." *Britannica*. **www.britannica.com/biography/Cicero.** Accessed 6 July 2020.

Matthew Lowther Clarke. "Quintilian." *Britannica*. **www.britannica.com/biography/Quintilian**. Accessed 6 July 2020.

James O'Donnell. "St. Augustine." *Britannica*. **www.britannica.com/biography/Saint-Augustine/Confessions**. Accessed 7 July 2020.

"Augustine on Christian Teaching." A podcast by *Mere Rhetoric*. **www.mererhetoric.libsyn.com/augustine-on-christian-teaching-new-and-improved.** Accessed 7 July 2020.

Richard Nordquist. "Renaissance rhetoric." *ThoughtCo*, 7 March 2017.

James Veazie Skalnik. *Ramus and Reform: University and Church at the End of the Renaissance*. Truman State University Press, 2002.

Bruce Herzberg & Patricia Bizzell. *The Rhetorical Tradition: Readings from Classical Times to the Present*. Bedford/St Martins, 1990.

"Locke's Rhetorical Theories." www.thelockedown.weebly.com/lockes-rhetoric.html. Accessed July 2020.

"History of Public Speaking." *Lumen Learning.* Boundless Communications. **www.courses.lumenlearning.com/boundless-communications/chapter/history-of-public-speaking/**. Accessed 8 July 2020.

Stephen Johnson. "7 of the greatest public speakers in history." *Big Think*, 5 September 2017. **www.bigthink.com/7-of-the-greatest-public-speakers-in-history.amp.html**. Accessed 8 July 2020.

A. Craig Baird. "Oratory." *Britannica*, **www.britannica.com/art/oratory-rhetoric.** Accessed 9 July 2020.

"Glossophobia." Merriam-Webstaer.com Dictionary, *Merriam-Webster*, **https://www.merriam-webster.com/dictionary/glossophobia**. Accessed 9 July 2020.

Lisa Fritscher. "Glossophobia or the Fear of Public Speaking." *Verywell Mind*, 12 April 2020. **www.verywellmind.com/glossophobia-2671860**. Accessed 9 July 2020.

Stephanie Faris. "Is Depression Genetic?" *Healthline*, 25 July 2017. **www.healthline.com/health/depression/genetic**. Accessed 9 July 2020.

Ellen Dunnigan. "The Very Real Science Behind your Fear of Public Speaking." *Accent On Business*, **www.accentonbusiness.net/the-very-real-science-behind-your-fear-of-public-speaking/.** Accessed 9 July 2020.

Zijing Sang. "What is Glossophobia?" *The Nerve Blog*, **https://sites.bu.edu/ombs/2017/11/27/what-is-glossophobia/**. Accessed 9 July 2020.

Suzanne Lachmann. "10 Sources of Low Self-Esteem." *Psychology Today*, 24 December 2013.

Arlin Cuncic. "Tips for Managing Public Speaking Anxiety." *Verywell Mind*, 24 February 2020. **www.verywellmind.com/tips-for-managing-public-speaking-anxiety-3024336**. Accessed 12 July 2020.

Dom Barnard. "What is Glossophobia and How to Overcome it." *Virtual Speech*, 18 November 2017. **www.virtualspeech.com/blog/what-is-glossophobia-and-how-to-overcome-it.** Accessed 12 July 2020.

Sheryl Ankrom. "Systematic Desensitization for Panic Disorders." *Verywell Mind*, 5 January 2020. **www.verywellmind.com/systematic-desensitization-2584317.** Accessed 12 July 2020.

Kendra Cherry. "What is Classical Conditioning?" *Verywell Mind*, 5 September 2020. **www.verywellmind.com/classical-conditioning-2794859**. Accessed 12 July 2020.

Arlin Cuncic. "Cognitive-Behavioral Therapy for Social Anxiety Disorder." *Verywell Mind*, 9 February 2020. **www.verywellmind.com/how-is-cbt-used-to-treat-sad-3024945.** Accessed 12 July 2020.

Scott Stossel. "Performance Anxiety in Great Performers." *The Atlantic*, January/February 2014 Issue.

Nayomi Chibana. "Amazing Leaders Who Once Had Stage Fright — And How They Overcame It." *Visme*. **www.visme.co/blog/amazing-leaders-who-once-had-crippling-stage-fright-and-how-they-overcame-it/**. Accessed 14 July 2020.

John Adams. *Diary and Autobiography of John Adams*, ed. L. H. Butterfield (Cambridge, MA: Harvard University Press, 1961), 3:335.

Brett & Kate McKay. "The Winston Churchill Guide to Public Speaking." *Art of Manliness*, 28 May 2015. **www.artofmanliness.com/articles/guide-to-public-speaking/**. Accessed 14 July 2020.

Kris Deichler. "Winston Churchill — His Struggle With Public Speaking." *Legends Report*. **www.legends.report/winston-churchill-his-struggle-with-public-speaking/.** Accessed 14 July 2020.

Abigail Gillibrand. "Julia Roberts and Harrison Ford lead long list of celebs who conquered public speaking fear." *Metro*, 15 October 2019.

Eileen Bailey. "Celebrities with Anxiety: Harrison Ford: Fear of Public Speaking." *Health Central*, 7 August 2008. **www.healthcentral.com/amp/article/celebrities-with-anxiety-harrison-ford-fear-of-public-speaking.** Accessed 14 July 2020.

Stephanie Sparer. "They're Just Like Us: How Celebrities Overcame Their Public Speaking Anxiety." beautiful.ai, **www.beautiful.ai/blog/celebrity-public-speaking-tips-anxiety.** Accessed 14 July 2020.

Amol Sarva. "How Julia Roberts Defeated Her Fear of Public Speaking." *Huffpost*, 6 December 2017.

Cátia Isabel Silva. "7 Famous People who fear Public Speaking." *The Virtual Orator*, 25 November 2019. **www.virtualorator.com/blog/7-famous-people-afraid-of-public-speaking/.** Accessed 15 July 2020.

Jenny Medeiros. "Richard Branson's Smart Strategy for Overcoming the Fear of Public Speaking." *Goalcast.* **www.goalcast.com/2018/06/05/richard-branson-overcome-public-speaking/amp/.** Accessed 15 July 2020.

Jeremy Quittner. "How Much Mark Cuban, Carly Fiorina, and Richard Branson Make in Speaking Fees." *Inc.* 11 February 2016.

Toastmasters International. "Harrison Ford and Julia Roberts Top List of Celebrities Who Found Success Despite a Fear of Public Speaking." *PR Newswire*, 15 October 2019. **www.prnewswire.com/news-releases/harrison-ford-and-julia-roberts-top-list-of-celebrities-who-found-success-despite-a-fear-of-public-speaking-300938384.html.** Accessed 16 July 2020.

Gary Genard. "Abraham Lincoln and Stage Fright: How to Overcome Fear of Public Speaking." *The Genard Method*, 3 August 2014. **www.genardmethod.com/blog/abraham-lincoln-and-stage-fright-how-to-overcome-fear-of-public-speaking.** Accessed 16 July 2020.

Carmine Gallo. "How Adele Is Managing Stage Fright." *Forbes*, 5 December 2015.

Stanford Encyclopedia of Philosophy. "Aristotle's Rhetoric." *Stanford Encyclopedia of Philosophy*, 2 May 2002. **www.plato.stanford.edu/entries/aristotle-rhetoric/#4.2.** Accessed 17 July 2020.

Barack Obama. "Remarks by the President in Address to the Nation on Syria." Office of the Press Secretary, The White House, 10 September 2013. **www.obamawhitehouse.archives.gov/the-press-office/2013/09/10/remarks-president-address-nation-syria.** Accessed 17 July 2020.

Amanda Macias. "Why Hitler was such as successful orator." *Business Insider*, 13 May 2015.

"Principles of Public Speaking." *Lumen Learning*. ER Services. **www.courses.lumenlearning.com/suny-publicspeakingprinciples/chapter/chapter-12-vocal-aspects-of-delivery/.** Accessed 18 July 2020.

Aristotle. *The Art of Rhetoric; With An English Translation by John Henry Freese*. London: William Heinemann. New York: G. P. Putnam's Sons.

"Aristotle Rhetoric 3." **www.perseus.tufts.edu/hopper/**

ABOUT THE AUTHOR

RON MALHOTRA is the author of five books, entrepreneur, award-winning wealth planner, success coach, business advisor, and thought-leadership mentor. Ron speaks internationally on topics including success, wealth, influence, and business. His views are highly sought after and have been published across a range of mainstream media. Ron's online content has been viewed more than fifty million times. Ron lives with his wife and daughter in Melbourne, Australia.

We hope you received tremendous value from Ron's book - *How To Speak Like The World's Top Public Speakers*. If you believe this book has been helpful, so you can become a better speaker, then please share your experience and 3 key learnings from the book with Ron, via email to **info@ronmalhotra.com**. Ron looks forward to hearing from you regarding your key learnings from the book.

If you loved *How To Speak Like The World's Top Public Speakers*, don't forget to check out Ron's other books, for many more insights, lessons, mental models and proven fundamental principles, so you can achieve success in all areas of your life.

Other titles by Ron:

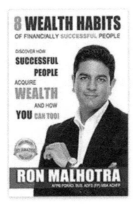

To learn more about Ron Malhotra,

visit **www.ronmalhotra.com**